CompTIA®
Network+
N10-006
Flash Cards and
Exam Practice Pack

Anthony Sequeira, CCIE No. 15626

D1520874

Pearson
800 East 96th Street
Indianapolis, IN 46240 USA

CompTIA Network+ N10-006 Flash Cards and Exam Practice Pack

Anthony Sequeira

Copyright © 2016 Pearson Education, Inc.

Printed in the United States of America

First Printing August 2015

Library of Congress Control Number: 2015942715

ISBN-13: 978-0-7897-5464-6

ISBN-10: 0-7897-5464-9

Trademark Acknowledgments

Warning and Disclaimer

Special Sales

For information about buying this title in bulk quantities, or for special sales opportunities (which may include electronic versions; custom cover designs; and content particular to your business, training goals, marketing focus, or branding interests), please contact our corporate sales department at corpsales@pearsoned.com or (800) 382-3419.

For government sales inquiries, please contact governmentsales@pearsoned.com.

For questions about sales outside the U.S., please contact international@pearsoned.com.

Publisher: Paul Boger	**Copy Editor:** Cheri Clark
Associate Publisher: Dave Dusthimer	**Technical Editor:** Sean Wilkins
Executive Editor: Brett Bartow	**Editorial Assistant:** Vanessa Evans
Managing Editor: Sandra Schroeder	**Cover Designer:** Mark Shirar
Development Editor: Marianne Bartow	**Composition:** Mary Sudul
Senior Project Editor: Tonya Simpson	**Proofreader:** Chuck Hutchinson

Contents at a Glance

About the Author

Anthony Sequeira, CCIE No. 15626, began his IT career in 1994 with IBM in Tampa, Florida. He quickly formed his own computer consultancy, Computer Solutions, and then discovered his true passion: teaching and writing about Microsoft and Cisco technologies. Anthony has lectured to massive audiences around the world while working for Mastering Computers. Anthony has never been happier in his career than he is now as a trainer for CBT Nuggets. He is an avid tennis player, a private pilot, and a semi-professional poker player, and he enjoys getting beaten up by women and children at the martial arts school he attends with his daughter.

About the Technical Reviewer

Sean Wilkins (@Sean_R_Wilkins) is an accomplished networking consultant and writer for infoDispersion (www.infodispersion.com) who has been in the IT field for more than 20 years, working with several large enterprises. Sean holds certifications with Cisco (CCNP/CCDP), Microsoft (MCSE), and CompTIA (A+ and Network+). His educational accomplishments include a Master of Science degree in information technology with a focus in network architecture and design, a Master of Science in organizational management, a Master certificate in network security, a Bachelor of Science in computer networking, and an Associate of Applied Science in computer information systems. Sean spends most of his time writing articles and books for various clients, including Cisco Press, Pearson, Tom's IT Pro, and PluralSight.

Dedications

This book is dedicated to my extended family at CBT Nuggets. Watch, learn, conquer!

Acknowledgments

Thanks so much, as always, to my friend Brett Bartow for this awesome opportunity. Thanks also to his beautiful wife, Marianne, for putting up with me.

This book would not have been possible without my dear friends Kevin Wallace and Keith Barker. Kevin, I am so proud of you and your amazing new venture. Keith, working with you every day at CBT Nuggets is a dream come true.

Thanks to Juliana, Jane, Ken, and all my friends at Slyce in Indian Rocks Beach who tolerated me night after night as I wrote this book. It sure is more fun than the local library—and open much later! Not to mention all the yummy Kentucky Bourbon Ale. And if you love pizza, it is THE place!

Thank you so much to my beautiful wife and daughter, Jo and Bella. Watching me sit in front of a computer is pretty drab, but helping people around the world realize better lives sure is worth the sacrifice. At least I hope you believe that.

Finally, thanks to Sean Wilkins for a killer technical edit. He is wicked smart.

We Want to Hear from You!

As the reader of this book, *you* are our most important critic and commentator. We value your opinion and want to know what we're doing right, what we could do better, what areas you'd like to see us publish in, and any other words of wisdom you're willing to pass our way.

We welcome your comments. You can email or write to let us know what you did or didn't like about this book—as well as what we can do to make our books better.

Please note that we cannot help you with technical problems related to the topic of this book.

When you write, please be sure to include this book's title and author as well as your name and email address. We will carefully review your comments and share them with the author and editors who worked on the book.

Email: feedback@pearsonitcertification.com

Mail: Pearson IT Certification
ATTN: Reader Feedback
800 East 96th Street
Indianapolis, IN 46240 USA

Reader Services

Visit our website and register this book at www.pearsonitcertification.com/register for convenient access to any updates, downloads, or errata that might be available for this book.

Introduction

Networking technologies are progressing at a breakneck pace and are becoming more crucial to corporations all the time. As such, the Network+ exam is more important than ever. As this text was written, much care was taken to follow the latest Network+ exam blueprint letter for letter. It was also written with the current and future state of networking in mind.

This text was designed to assist you very directly with your Network+ exam. The primary tool here is the Flash Cards, which were created to ensure your quick recall of the many facts and rich vocabulary of modern networking.

Using Flash Cards

Flash Cards have been a proven method of learning everything from anatomy for medical students to learning a new language.

Because many compare mastering Network+ to learning a new language, these tools are perfect to assist you in your journey to conquering the Network+ exam.

Care was taken to construct the Flash Cards in a manner most conducive to your learning. A brief query is composed on the front of the card, and then a verified correct answer is on the back of the card. Some Flash Cards could have more than one correct response. In that case, we provided as many examples of correct answers as possible.

We organized the Flash Cards to coordinate with the Network+ study blueprint to maximize their effectiveness. So, for example, if you are feeling weak in the area of wireless LANs, you can go directly to that section of the Flash Cards.

Review the cards as many times as necessary to feel confident in each area of study. It is recommended that you review all cards one final time before the actual test.

Using the Quick Reference Sheets

Another excellent tool is the Quick Reference Sheets. These not only will serve to refresh you in key exam blueprint areas, but also will serve as a quick reference when you are working in or designing modern networks. You can use the Flash Card section to help determine areas where you might need additional review.

Although the Quick Reference Sheets are not meant to provide exhaustive coverage of the material in each blueprint section, they are guaranteed to review *every* topic mentioned. This ensures that there are no unpleasant surprises in your Network+ exam.

You should consider further research in areas where you might need additional assistance or in areas that you are interested in. Let these Quick Reference Sheets provide you with a strong foundation of knowledge in these topics that you can easily build on using resources such as Safari Books Online or Wikipedia.

What's On the CD-ROM?

The CD-ROM that accompanies this book is also very valuable. When you are ready to test your knowledge, the disc contains hundreds of multiple-choice questions for practice, as well as dozens of performance-based questions that mimic those found in the actual exam. These exercises should prove to be very challenging.

It is critical that you study with these resources before your exam. Although the Flash Cards and Quick Reference Sheets are incredibly important study tools, they are not presented in the format you will encounter on the exam. Working with the resources on the CD-ROM will not only further your understanding of what you truly do not know, but also help you to feel confident with the format of questions in your actual exam.

Chapter 1
Network Devices and Services

QUESTION 1

What is an example of a Class A private IP address?

QUESTION 2

What type of address is a switch most concerned with?

QUESTION 3

What type of firewall can dynamically permit return traffic based on observed outgoing traffic?

ANSWER 1

10.10.10.1

ANSWER 2

MAC address

ANSWER 3

Stateful firewall

QUESTION 4

What type of intrusion prevention system is installed on a client machine?

QUESTION 5

What type of network security device attempts to prevent unwanted traffic from entering your network based on signatures?

QUESTION 6

What device is wired or wireless and is often the device through which your employees access the Internet?

ANSWER 4

Host Intrusion Prevention System (HIPS)

ANSWER 5

Intrusion Prevention System (IPS)

ANSWER 6

Access point or wireless router

QUESTION 7

How are you able to access a firewall on the network initially?

QUESTION 8

What type of VPN permits devices to easily connect through another device at each end of the connection?

QUESTION 9

What two IPsec elements can be used for authentication?

ANSWER 7

The default web access IP address and credentials or the local console port

ANSWER 8

Site-to-site VPN

ANSWER 9

MD5, SHA-1

QUESTION 10

What three IPsec elements can be used for encryption?

QUESTION 11

What VPN technology permits the use of a standard web browser as the VPN client?

QUESTION 12

What two security communication protocols are often used in AAA?

ANSWER 10

DES, 3DES, AES

ANSWER 11

SSL VPN

ANSWER 12

TACACS, RADIUS

QUESTION 13

Why is TACACS often considered more secure than RADIUS?

QUESTION 14

What service might you use to connect to a remote Windows Server 2012 system over the Internet?

QUESTION 15

In addition to the installation of HIPS on your employees' systems, what might help with the prevention of malware problems?

ANSWER 13

TACACS encrypts the entire packet.

ANSWER 14

RAS

ANSWER 15

Options include IPS, firewalls, and employee education.

Chapter 2

Configuring Network Services

Chapter 2
Configuring Network Services

QUESTION 1

How does a client with no IP address configuration find a local DHCP server?

QUESTION 2

How do you assign information such as default gateway and DNS addresses with DHCP?

QUESTION 3

What DHCP configuration approach might be perfect for assigning an address to a network printer?

ANSWER 1

A broadcast packet

ANSWER 2

Options

ANSWER 3

Reservation

QUESTION 4

What DHCP configuration dictates how long a client can retain its IP address information?

QUESTION 5

What are the four steps of the DHCP process?

QUESTION 6

Why is a DHCP Relay Agent often needed in a network?

ANSWER 4

Lease duration

ANSWER 5

Discover, Offer, Request, Acknowledgment

ANSWER 6

The client Discover message is a broadcast, and broadcasts are not forwarded by routers.

QUESTION 7

What is a domain name alias record in DNS?

QUESTION 8

What is an MX record used for in DNS?

QUESTION 9

What is a server (a computer system or an application) that acts as an intermediary for requests from clients seeking resources from other servers?

ANSWER 7

A CNAME record

ANSWER 8

To point to a mail server

ANSWER 9

A proxy server

QUESTION 10

What service is used to enable private addresses to communicate on public networks?

QUESTION 11

What is SNAT?

QUESTION 12

How can many internal, private addresses use a single public address for translation?

ANSWER 10

NAT

ANSWER 11

Static Network Address Translation—this is the manual assignment of an address translation.

ANSWER 12

Port Address Translation (PAT)

QUESTION 13

What capability can assist you in directing external clients to an internal Web server in your private network?

QUESTION 14

Provide three examples of private addresses.

QUESTION 15

What type of DNS record is used for an IPv4 host?

ANSWER 13

Port forwarding

ANSWER 14

Any valid address from the following ranges: 10.0.0.0–10.255.255.255; 172.16.0.0–172.31.255.255; 192.168.0.0–192.168.255.255

ANSWER 15

An A record

Chapter 3
WAN Technologies

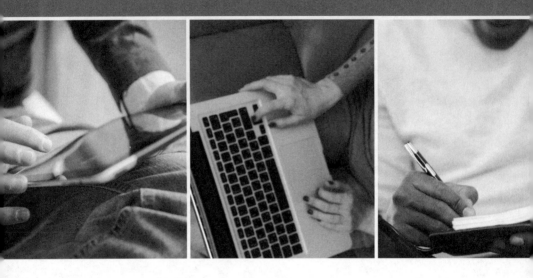

Chapter 3
WAN Technologies

QUESTION 1

Which fiber technology systems must maintain more stable wavelength or frequency than those needed for CWDM because of the closer spacing of the wavelengths?

QUESTION 2

What would you call a minimum bandwidth guarantee in Frame Relay?

QUESTION 3

What two WAN technologies would be good for rural areas?

ANSWER 1

Dense wavelength division multiplexing (DWDM)

ANSWER 2

Committed information rate (CIR)

ANSWER 3

Satellite and WiMAX

QUESTION 4

What WAN technology uses frequency ranges of 5 MHz to 42 MHz upstream and 50 MHz to 860 MHz downstream?

QUESTION 5

What is an excellent high-speed DSL option?

QUESTION 6

How many B channels does ISDN PRI have?

ANSWER 4

Broadband cable

ANSWER 5

Very-high-bit-rate DSL (VDSL)

ANSWER 6

The ISDN PRI circuit has 23 B channels.

QUESTION 7

How is a virtual path labeled in ATM?

QUESTION 8

Name three PPP authentication options.

QUESTION 9

How big is the header and label in MPLS?

ANSWER 7

Virtual path identifier (VPI)

ANSWER 8

PAP, CHAP, and MS-CHAP

ANSWER 9

A 32-bit header is used with a 20-bit label.

QUESTION 10

How is label switching more efficient than traditional forwarding technologies?

QUESTION 11

A T1 or T3 would be an example of what type of WAN technology?

QUESTION 12

Which has a higher capacity, E1 or T1?

ANSWER 10

Layer 3 lookups are avoided.

ANSWER 11

Dedicated leased line

ANSWER 12

The E1; it has a bandwidth capacity of 2.048 Mbps.

QUESTION 13

What is a digital modem that is often used in a dedicated leased line environment?

QUESTION 14

What is an example of a cell-switched technology?

QUESTION 15

What is an example of a circuit-switched technology?

ANSWER 13

Channel service unit/data service unit (CSU/DSU)

ANSWER 14

ATM

ANSWER 15

ISDN

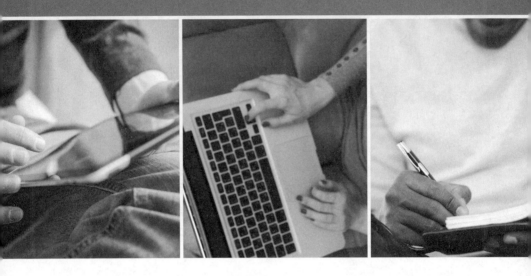

Chapter 4

Install Cables and Connectors

QUESTION 1

What category of UTP is often used for 10 Mbps Ethernet?

QUESTION 2

What category of UTP is often used for Fast Ethernet?

QUESTION 3

What two categories of UTP are used for 1 Gbps Ethernet?

ANSWER 1

Cat 3

ANSWER 2

Cat 5

ANSWER 3

Cat 5e, Cat 6

QUESTION 4

What category of UTP is often used for 10 Gbps Ethernet?

QUESTION 5

What type of twisted-pair cabling can be used where fire is a concern?

QUESTION 6

What feature permits your device to automatically adjust to the type of cable connected (straight-through or crossover)?

ANSWER 4

Cat 6a

ANSWER 5

Plenum cabling

ANSWER 6

Auto-MDIX

QUESTION 7

What type of cable would you use to connect to the console port of a router or switch?

QUESTION 8

What is an eight-pin connector found in most Ethernet networks?

QUESTION 9

What is often used to connect coaxial cables back to back?

ANSWER 7

Rollover cable

ANSWER 8

A type 45 registered jack (RJ-45)

ANSWER 9

BNC/BNC coupler

QUESTION 10

What media type eliminates the issue of multimode delay distortion by having a core with a diameter so small that it permits only one mode (that is, one path) of propagation?

QUESTION 11

What would you use to attach a connector (RJ-45) to an Ethernet cable?

QUESTION 12

What tool would you use to determine exactly where a break in a cable is located?

ANSWER 10

Single-mode fiber

ANSWER 11

Crimper

ANSWER 12

TDR

QUESTION 13

What tool can you use to determine what category of cable you are working with?

QUESTION 14

What color is used for pin 1 with the T568A color standard?

QUESTION 15

What color is used for pin 1 with the T568B color standard?

ANSWER 13

Cable certifier

ANSWER 14

White/green stripe

ANSWER 15

White/orange stripe

Chapter 5
Network Topologies and Infrastructures

QUESTION 1

What type of network uses $n(n - 1) / 2$ to calculate the number of connections you need?

QUESTION 2

What type of network features a balance between the number of connections for high availability and the ease of admin?

QUESTION 3

What network topology was used in early Ethernet networks?

ANSWER 1

Full mesh

ANSWER 2

Partial mesh

ANSWER 3

Bus

QUESTION 4

What topology was used in FDDI networks?

QUESTION 5

What topology do you often find in an Ethernet network today?

QUESTION 6

If two systems are connected with a WAN link, what topology is this?

ANSWER 4

Ring

ANSWER 5

Star

ANSWER 6

Point-to-point

QUESTION 7

If one device is doing most of the processing and overhead, your device setup is called what?

QUESTION 8

What does MAN stand for when describing a network?

QUESTION 9

What does PAN stand for when describing a network?

ANSWER 7

Client-server

ANSWER 8

Metropolitan-area network

ANSWER 9

Personal area network

QUESTION 10

In the star topology, what happens if there is a break between a node and the central device?

QUESTION 11

Where do you often find a SCADA network?

QUESTION 12

What is a medianet used for?

ANSWER 10

Only that node is affected.

ANSWER 11

In industrial areas

ANSWER 12

A medianet is a network optimized for the transport of rich audio and video traffic.

QUESTION 13

Bluetooth and IR are often used in what type of network?

QUESTION 14

If you are in a Windows workgroup, you are in what type of network?

QUESTION 15

In a ring topology, what happens if there is a break in the ring?

ANSWER 13

PAN

ANSWER 14

Peer-to-peer

ANSWER 15

All devices can be impacted.

Chapter 6
Addressing Schemes

QUESTION 1

How long is an IPv6 address?

QUESTION 2

What technique is commonly used to assign the low-order bits of an IPv6 address?

QUESTION 3

How does a link-local IPv6 address typically begin?

ANSWER 1

128 bits

ANSWER 2

Extended Unique Identifier (EUI-64)

ANSWER 3

FE80

QUESTION 4

What are the two rules for shortening the format of an IPv6 address?

QUESTION 5

What IPv6 transition technology aimed at host computers can perform its function even from behind Network Address Translation (NAT) devices such as home routers?

QUESTION 6

What are the Class A, B, and C private address ranges?

ANSWER 4

Leading 0s in a field can be omitted; contiguous fields of zeros can be represented as :: once in an address.

ANSWER 5

Teredo tunneling

ANSWER 6

10.0.0.0–10.255.255.255

172.16.0.0–172.31.255.255

192.168.0.0–192.168.255.255

QUESTION 7

What is the default mask for a Class B IPv4 network?

QUESTION 8

What type of IPv4 or IPv6 transmission targets a group of receivers that have indicated they are interested in the traffic?

QUESTION 9

What is the APIPA range of addresses?

ANSWER 7

255.255.0.0

ANSWER 8

Multicast

ANSWER 9

169.254.0.0/16

QUESTION 10

What is the formula for the number of hosts that can be assigned in a subnet?

QUESTION 11

What is the formula for the number of subnets that you can create given a number of bits?

QUESTION 12

What is the usable address range for the third subnet of 192.168.10.0/27?

ANSWER 10

2 raised to the x minus 2, where x is the number of host bits.

ANSWER 11

2 raised to the x, where x is the number of borrowed bits.

ANSWER 12

192.168.10.65–192.168.10.94

QUESTION 13

What is the process involved in CIDR?

QUESTION 14

What is it called if your interface runs both IPv4 and IPv6?

QUESTION 15

What technology features identical IPv6 addresses assigned to multiple interfaces?

ANSWER 13

Borrowing bits from the network portion of the address, also called route aggregation or super-netting

ANSWER 14

Dual stack

ANSWER 15

Anycast

Chapter 7

Routing Concepts

QUESTION 1

What is the IP address space reserved for loopback addressing?

QUESTION 2

What routing loop prevention mechanism prohibits a router from sending an update out an interface where it originally learned the update?

QUESTION 3

What are the three methods by which a route prefix can make it into the routing table on a router?

ANSWER 1

Used for testing purposes mainly, it is the 127.0.0.0 address space.

ANSWER 2

Split horizon

ANSWER 3

The route is directly connected to the router, the route is placed there statically by an administrator, or the route is learned dynamically from a routing protocol.

QUESTION 4

What is the form (IP address and mask) of a default route on a router?

QUESTION 5

What type of dynamic routing protocol is often termed as routing by rumor?

QUESTION 6

What routing protocol uses hop count as its metric?

ANSWER 4

0.0.0.0/0

ANSWER 5

Distance vector

ANSWER 6

RIP

QUESTION 7

What is the EGP used by the Internet and many large corporations?

QUESTION 8

What are two examples of link-state routing protocols?

QUESTION 9

Moving OSPF learned routes into the RIPv2 process on a router would be known as what?

ANSWER 7

Border Gateway Protocol (BGP)

ANSWER 8

IS-IS, OSPF

ANSWER 9

Route redistribution

QUESTION 10

What is an open-standard version of HSRP?

QUESTION 11

In an HSRP group, what is the name of the router that is actually forwarding the traffic, and the name of the backup device?

QUESTION 12

What is the admin distance for a directly connected route?

ANSWER 10

VRRP

ANSWER 11

The forwarder is termed the active router and the backup is termed the standby router.

ANSWER 12

0

QUESTION 13

What is the admin distance for a statically configured route?

QUESTION 14

What is the admin distance for RIPv2?

QUESTION 15

What is the admin distance for OSPF?

ANSWER 13

1

ANSWER 14

120

ANSWER 15

110

Chapter 8

Unified Communications Technologies

QUESTION 1

What three forms of traffic might you find on a unified communications network?

QUESTION 2

What is the traditional privately owned switch for a voice network?

QUESTION 3

What is the typical endpoint in a VoIP network for voice?

ANSWER 1

Data, voice, video

ANSWER 2

A PBX

ANSWER 3

An IP phone

QUESTION 4

What unified communications component analyzes dialed digits and determines how to route the call?

QUESTION 5

What is a VoIP signaling protocol that is used to set up, maintain, and tear down calls?

QUESTION 6

What protocol is often used to carry voice traffic?

ANSWER 4

A call agent

ANSWER 5

SIP

ANSWER 6

RTP

QUESTION 7

What is a variation in delay in QoS?

QUESTION 8

What QoS method uses strictly a FIFO approach?

QUESTION 9

What protocol is responsible for creating, maintaining, and tearing down video sessions on the network?

ANSWER 7

Jitter

ANSWER 8

Best-Effort

ANSWER 9

SIP

QUESTION 10

What component (technology) in a unified communications network is responsible for converting from analog to digital or from digital to analog?

QUESTION 11

What QoS marking is often used at Layer 2?

QUESTION 12

What QoS marking is often used at Layer 3?

ANSWER 10

Codec

ANSWER 11

CoS

ANSWER 12

DSCP

QUESTION 13

What QoS tools seek to smooth out traffic flows?

QUESTION 14

What type of QoS tool is compression?

QUESTION 15

What are two categories of congestion control in DiffServ QoS?

ANSWER 13

Traffic shaping

ANSWER 14

A link efficiency tool

ANSWER 15

Congestion management and congestion avoidance

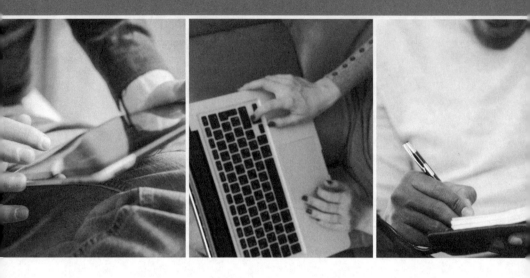

Chapter 9

Cloud and Virtualization

QUESTION 1

What is the term for a server that is running on a single hardware platform next to many other servers?

QUESTION 2

What might provide security between virtual servers and the rest of the network infrastructure?

QUESTION 3

In the VMware environment, virtual servers can connect to the network through what device?

ANSWER 1

Virtual server

ANSWER 2

Virtual firewall

ANSWER 3

Virtual switch

QUESTION 4

What technology permits a user to have her GUI interface for using her device delivered to her out of a central repository?

QUESTION 5

What is the term for having your data center provided by a service provider and then billed per usage?

QUESTION 6

Your company rents virtualized servers (which are hosted by a service provider) and then runs specific applications on those servers. What is this called?

ANSWER 4

Virtual desktop

ANSWER 5

NaaS

ANSWER 6

IaaS

QUESTION 7

You are using cloud services in which the details of the servers are hidden from the customer and the customer's experience is similar to using a web-based application. What is this called?

QUESTION 8

Your company developers are busy creating applications and want to focus on creating the software without having to worry about the servers and infrastructure that are being used for that development. What is this cloud service called?

QUESTION 9

If you have an engineer in your company who is able to configure all aspects of the network using a simple GUI, it might be what technology?

ANSWER 7

SaaS

ANSWER 8

PaaS

ANSWER 9

Software defined networking

QUESTION 10

What is the term used for your cloud infrastructure if you build it all, or have it built for you, and it is all maintained within your organization and is not shared with any other entity?

QUESTION 11

What type of cloud technology might be free, and might involve substantially different security concerns than a private cloud?

QUESTION 12

What is it called when your cloud infrastructure combines the features of two or more other cloud designs?

ANSWER 10

Private cloud

ANSWER 11

Public cloud

ANSWER 12

Hybrid cloud

QUESTION 13

What are two advantages of using a virtualized infrastructure?

QUESTION 14

Name the leader in virtualization technologies.

QUESTION 15

AWS, Google, and Microsoft all offer which cloud option?

ANSWER 13

Lower TCO, better use of hardware resources

ANSWER 14

VMware

ANSWER 15

Public cloud

Chapter 10

Implement a Basic Network

QUESTION 1

What is the term for the measure of how quickly and easily your network can grow as needed?

QUESTION 2

When planning for device requirements, what three business forces might factor in?

QUESTION 3

What four environmental limitations might impact you when you're implementing a basic network?

ANSWER 1

Scalability

ANSWER 2

ROI, regulations, competitiveness

ANSWER 3

Power, temperature, humidity, wireless interference

QUESTION 4

What four equipment limitations might you encounter when implementing a basic network?

QUESTION 5

Name three considerations in deciding between wired and wireless networking.

ANSWER 4

Performance, redundancy limitations, management limitations, upgradeability limitations

ANSWER 5

Options include security, performance, scalability, availability, and cost.

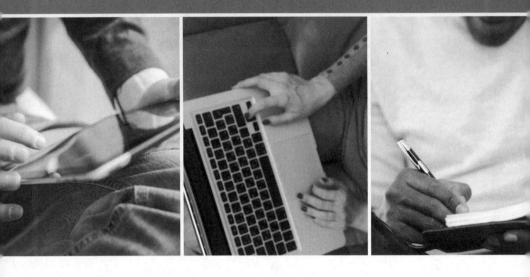

Chapter 11

Monitoring Tools

QUESTION 1

You need to search for a specific data string in a packet entering your network. You cannot currently afford an IPS/IDS system or a firewall. What could you use?

QUESTION 2

What version of SNMP features few security enhancements but did feature 64-bit counters for monitoring?

QUESTION 3

What version of SNMP is known for its massive security enhancements?

ANSWER 1

Packet/network analyzer

ANSWER 2

SNMP 2c

ANSWER 3

SNMP 3

QUESTION 4

What SNMP message is sent from a monitored system in response to some threshold being crossed?

QUESTION 5

What is the database referred to that exists on a monitored system for interrogation by SNMP?

QUESTION 6

You need to send status updates, warnings, and other alerts from many network devices to a central location. You are not interested in SNMP usage. What service can you call upon for this purpose?

ANSWER 4

Trap

ANSWER 5

MIB (management information base)

ANSWER 6

SYSLOG

QUESTION 7

What does SIEM stand for in the context of networking?

QUESTION 8

You are interested in enhancing the security of your network environment by implementing a system that permits access only to devices that are at a certain antivirus and patch level. What system should you consider?

QUESTION 9

What is the term for a collection of metrics regarding your network during typical, everyday, common usage?

ANSWER 7

Security information and event management

ANSWER 8

Network Admission Control (NAC)

ANSWER 9

Baseline

QUESTION 10

What is a term for a bandwidth shortage location in your network, commonly due to a dramatic increase in usage in that segment?

QUESTION 11

An attacker is performing a reconnaissance attack against your network. He is trying to determine what services are listening for traffic. What tool is he most likely using?

QUESTION 12

What are two common areas that an environmental monitoring tool would be monitoring?

ANSWER 10

Bottleneck

ANSWER 11

Port scanner

ANSWER 12

Temperature, humidity levels

QUESTION 13

A duplex mismatch would most likely produce what behavior?

QUESTION 14

What SNMP message is sent from a management system to a managed device in order to obtain a reading on a variable?

QUESTION 15

What ports are used by SNMP?

ANSWER 13

Unreliable communications, not total communications loss

ANSWER 14

GET

ANSWER 15

161, 162

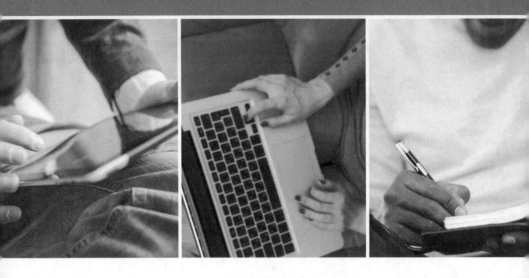

Chapter 12

Network Segmentation

QUESTION 1

Your CIO has asked you to implement a new NAC system in your company for controlling mobile device access. Where should you implement this new solution first?

QUESTION 2

What does SCADA stand for in information technology?

QUESTION 3

If a Windows XP system was still operating in your IT infrastructure, what would it be referred to as?

ANSWER 1

In a test lab

ANSWER 2

Supervisory Control and Data Acquisition

ANSWER 3

A legacy system

QUESTION 4

What are three major concerns with legacy systems?

QUESTION 5

What type of addressing is often found in a private network segment?

QUESTION 6

What technology can be used to create multiple subnets off of a single switch?

ANSWER 4

Compatibility with new technology, vendor support, security vulnerabilities

ANSWER 5

RFC 1918 addressing

ANSWER 6

Virtual local area networks (VLAN)

QUESTION 7

What technology seeks to make a network look vulnerable to attacks?

QUESTION 8

What variation of IPS seeks to represent a vulnerable network device?

QUESTION 9

DNS can be used to distribute traffic among multiple servers. This is a form of what segmentation technique?

ANSWER 7

Honey network

ANSWER 8

Honeypot

ANSWER 9

Load balancing

QUESTION 10

Traffic such as gaming and social media traffic is often categorized into what grouping in a corporation?

QUESTION 11

What are three big advantages of VLAN segmentation?

QUESTION 12

If you must create a new private network segment following strict security guidelines based on a government mandate, this is an example of what area of IT?

ANSWER 10

Scavenger

ANSWER 11

Reduced broadcast domains, security through segmentation, increased flexibility

ANSWER 12

Regulatory compliance

QUESTION 13

Unauthorized DHCP servers that are present in your organization are referred to as what?

QUESTION 14

What security issue harms networks by replicating across infected computers, never attaching themselves to specific files or programs?

QUESTION 15

What is needed to move traffic between virtual local area networks?

ANSWER 13

Rogue

ANSWER 14

Worms

ANSWER 15

An RP (Route Processor)

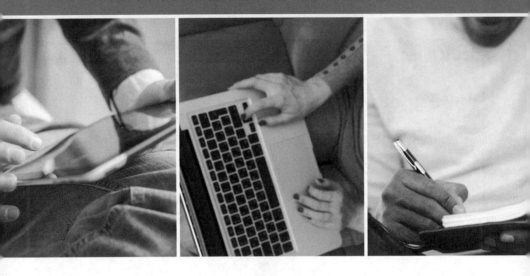

Chapter 13

Patches and Updates

QUESTION 1

What type of segmentation might be excellent when there is a major update to an operating system that is ready from a vendor?

QUESTION 2

OS updates are often broken into what two categories?

QUESTION 3

What might break following a major OS update?

ANSWER 1

A testing lab

ANSWER 2

Major and minor updates

ANSWER 3

Applications

QUESTION 4

What Windows feature controls enhancements and fixes to the OS and some apps?

QUESTION 5

You have implemented new drivers that are not working correctly in your environment; what should be your first attempt at fixing this problem?

QUESTION 6

What Windows feature is designed as a "last-ditch" effort tool for restoring a system to a running state?

ANSWER 4

Windows Update

ANSWER 5

Roll back the drivers

ANSWER 6

Last Known Good Configuration

QUESTION 7

If you remove a firmware update that you applied, restoring the previous version, what is this called?

QUESTION 8

What should be a key initial step before you upgrade a system after testing the upgrade in a test lab?

QUESTION 9

What should you read before upgrading a system with a major update?

ANSWER 7

Rollback

ANSWER 8

Back up the configuration

ANSWER 9

The release notes

QUESTION 10

What is critical before a vulnerability patch is implemented across your organization?

QUESTION 11

There is an update available for your system's video. What type of update is this most likely?

QUESTION 12

What is the combination of a hardware device, for example, an integrated circuit, and computer instructions and data that reside as read-only software on that device? As a result, it usually cannot be modified during normal operation of the device.

ANSWER 10

A testing lab

ANSWER 11

A driver update

ANSWER 12

Firmware

QUESTION 13

Windows enables you to "ignore" an update that might cause harm to your system. What is this referred to as in Windows Update?

QUESTION 14

Why might you choose never to install Windows Updates?

QUESTION 15

A major OS update might require what after the successful company-wide rollout?

ANSWER 13

Hide Update

ANSWER 14

Because you cannot risk impacting mission-critical applications

ANSWER 15

User training and/or documentation updating

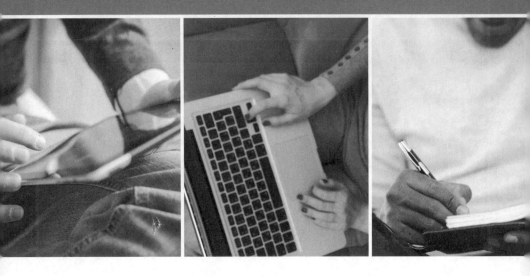

Chapter 14

Implementing Switches

QUESTION 1

What is the default VLAN used by Cisco switches?

QUESTION 2

You run the **show vlan brief** command and you notice that some ports are not listed in the output. Why is this most likely?

QUESTION 3

What are the two main modes of a port on a Cisco switch?

ANSWER 1

VLAN 1

ANSWER 2

The ports are trunks.

ANSWER 3

Access and trunk

QUESTION 4

Your Cisco switch is configured with three VLANs in addition to the default VLAN you are using for management traffic. How many broadcast domains are on the switch?

QUESTION 5

What are the two Power over Ethernet standards?

QUESTION 6

What Cisco technology enables you to synchronize your VLANs across devices?

ANSWER 4

Four

ANSWER 5

802.3af and 802.3at

ANSWER 6

VTP

QUESTION 7

Why would you assign a default gateway to a Layer 2 switch?

QUESTION 8

Instead of using the local username database on your switches, you want to rely on an external database for tracking access and also authenticating and verifying what commands are possible. What system should you use?

QUESTION 9

What is a standards-based method of tagging traffic based on VLAN assignments?

ANSWER 7

So that the switch can respond to management traffic originated from a remote subnet

ANSWER 8

AAA

ANSWER 9

802.1Q

QUESTION 10

Why might you choose to use an unmanaged switch in your network?

QUESTION 11

What standards-based protocol allows you to bundle links together on a switch to increase available bandwidth and to add redundancy?

QUESTION 12

What interface is used to assign an IP address to a VLAN?

ANSWER 10

It is less expensive.

ANSWER 11

LACP

ANSWER 12

An SVI (switched virtual interface)

QUESTION 13

How many virtual terminal interfaces are found on a Cisco switch by default, and what are their numbers?

QUESTION 14

What is the official standard designator for classic STP?

QUESTION 15

What newer version of STP seeks to reduce convergence time?

ANSWER 13

There are five interfaces numbered 0 through 4. More can be added, and all can be assigned special properties and controls.

ANSWER 14

802.1D

ANSWER 15

802.1w, or rapid spanning tree protocol

Chapter 15

Implement a Wireless LAN

QUESTION 1

A wireless router for the SOHO often features what technology for internal devices in addition to the routing and wireless functions?

QUESTION 2

Device density on an AP refers to what?

QUESTION 3

What are two options for a communication protocol between access points and a wireless LAN controller?

ANSWER 1

Switching

ANSWER 2

The number of clients associated with the AP

ANSWER 3

LWAPP or CAPWAP

QUESTION 4

What can be used to connect very remote clients to an AP in a wireless LAN?

QUESTION 5

What would measure the signals being generated by the access points to confirm there is adequate coverage for wireless networking in the desired areas?

QUESTION 6

What are the two major frequency groups used by wireless?

ANSWER 4

A wireless bridge, or repeater, or extender

ANSWER 5

A site survey

ANSWER 6

2.4 GHz and 5 GHz

QUESTION 7

What are the nonoverlapping channels in the 2.4 GHz range in the United States?

QUESTION 8

What is the application layer throughput after the overhead of an underlying protocol is taken away?

QUESTION 9

What is a common directional wireless antenna?

ANSWER 7

1, 6, and 11

ANSWER 8

Goodput

ANSWER 9

Yagi

QUESTION 10

Which wireless standard supports MU-MIMO?

ANSWER 10

802.11ac

Chapter 16

Network Security Overview

QUESTION 1

Your boss has indicated that you need to set up an archive of mission-critical data that is accessible from the main office. He wants this located in a different continent. What part of planning is he working with?

QUESTION 2

What is a key element in protecting against social engineering attacks?

QUESTION 3

If your security tool is scanning for open ports or unprotected services, it is engaged in what element of security?

ANSWER 1

Disaster recovery planning

ANSWER 2

Employee training

ANSWER 3

Vulnerability scanning

QUESTION 4

To check the effectiveness of your company's security policy and technologies, you might engage in what practice?

QUESTION 5

A botnet is used in what type of security attack?

QUESTION 6

What type of attack would attempt to corrupt the Layer 2 information learned by a device?

ANSWER 4

Penetration testing

ANSWER 5

A Distributed Denial of Service (DDoS) attack

ANSWER 6

ARP cache poisoning

QUESTION 7

If an attacker is lying about the source IP address, this is known as what type of an attack?

QUESTION 8

If an unsolicited message is sent to your Bluetooth device, this is known as what type of attack?

QUESTION 9

If an attacker calls one of your employees pretending to be with IT, this is an example of what type of attack?

ANSWER 7

Spoofing

ANSWER 8

Bluejacking

ANSWER 9

Social engineering

QUESTION 10

Capturing packets that are being sent between two network devices in an unencrypted fashion is an example of what attack?

ANSWER 10

Man-in-the-middle

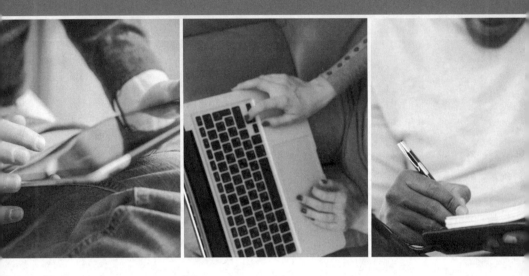

Chapter 17
Network Hardening

QUESTION 1

What is an umbrella term used for software that is intended to damage or harm computers?

QUESTION 2

If your switch port is configured with port security and you would like to use a computer and an IP phone on the port, how many MAC addresses should port security permit?

QUESTION 3

What security feature is designed to guard against rogue DHCP servers directly?

ANSWER 1

Malware

ANSWER 2

Two

ANSWER 3

DHCP snooping

QUESTION 4

An attacker in your network keeps exhausting switch tables in an attempt to capture traffic between devices. What is this attack commonly termed?

QUESTION 5

What should you consider combining with the dissemination of portions of your company security policy?

QUESTION 6

Provide a secure alternative for each of the following protocols: HTTP, SNMP v2C, Telnet.

ANSWER 4

A MAC flooding attack

ANSWER 5

Employee training

ANSWER 6

HTTPS, SNMP v3, SSH

QUESTION 7

Your colleague created an access list and applied it correctly to a router interface. Even though he has a deny statement for a specific form of traffic from a host machine in place, the traffic is still permitted. Provide a reason why.

QUESTION 8

What technology permits the use of a web browser as a VPN client?

QUESTION 9

MD5 and SHA are examples of what?

ANSWER 7

The order of the statements in the list is not correct; there is an earlier statement permitting the traffic in the list.

ANSWER 8

SSL/TLS

ANSWER 9

Hashing algorithms

QUESTION 10

Your peer configured your firewall and there are problems. You cannot determine the IP address he used for management purposes. What might you do?

ANSWER 10

Reset the firewall to factory defaults and use the default management address.

Chapter 18
Network Troubleshooting
Methodologies

QUESTION 1

If you begin troubleshooting a problem by seeing whether the device has power, you are using what common method?

QUESTION 2

After you have validated that you have resolved a major problem in your network, what might you do next?

QUESTION 3

What troubleshooting method would start at the application layer of the OSI model?

ANSWER 1

Bottom up

ANSWER 2

Update documentation

ANSWER 3

Top down

QUESTION 4

What is a troubleshooting method that has you start at any layer of the OSI model depending on your initial testing?

QUESTION 5

Gathering information is done early with a network issue. What is the main purpose of this step?

ANSWER 4

Divide and conquer

ANSWER 5

To identify the actual problem

Chapter 19

Network Troubleshooting Tools

QUESTION 1

What command-line utility in Windows permits you to release and renew DHCP information?

QUESTION 2

You want to see incoming and outgoing network connections from the command line on your Linux machine. What tool should you use?

QUESTION 3

You are on a UNIX system and you would like to view details about the IP address and parameters of an interface. What command should you use?

ANSWER 1

ipconfig

ANSWER 2

netstat

ANSWER 3

ifconfig

QUESTION 4

What protocol does ping rely on?

QUESTION 5

What command-line tool should you use to verify the path that traffic is taking through the network?

QUESTION 6

What Windows command-line tool permits you to verify the specifics of DNS name resolution?

ANSWER 4

Internet Control Message Protocol (ICMP)

ANSWER 5

Traceroute or tracert

ANSWER 6

nslookup

QUESTION 7

What command-line tool in Windows permits the inspection of NetBIOS name resolution?

QUESTION 8

What command-line tool permits the analysis of cached Layer 2 information?

QUESTION 9

What switch can you use with ipconfig to view the most detail?

ANSWER 7

nbtstat

ANSWER 8

arp

ANSWER 9

/all

QUESTION 10

Ping enables you to view reachability information and also provides what?

ANSWER 10

Basic information about latency

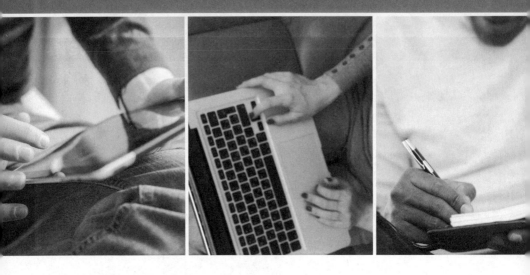

Chapter 20
Troubleshooting Wireless and Copper

QUESTION 1

What are the three nonoverlapping channels in the 2.4 GHz range in the U.S.?

QUESTION 2

What is commonly referred to as the "network name" in wireless networking?

QUESTION 3

What is the term for an unauthorized access point in your organization?

ANSWER 1

1, 6, and 11

ANSWER 2

SSID (service set identifier)

ANSWER 3

Rogue access point

QUESTION 4

If you need to send wireless information from building to building, what type of antenna would you use?

QUESTION 5

What are some devices that have been known to cause interference with wireless devices?

QUESTION 6

MU-MIMO is used in what wireless technology?

ANSWER 4

A unidirectional antenna; for example, a Yagi antenna

ANSWER 5

Cordless phones, microwaves, wireless gaming

ANSWER 6

802.11ac

QUESTION 7

MIMO was created for what wireless technology group?

QUESTION 8

What protocol is commonly used to communicate between an AP and a wireless controller?

QUESTION 9

What environmental factors can often impact wireless networking?

ANSWER 7

802.11n

ANSWER 8

Lightweight Access Point Protocol (LWAPP)

ANSWER 9

Concrete walls, window film, filing cabinets, metal studs, or chicken wire in walls

QUESTION 10

You are using a cable tester and you have verified that pin 1 connects to pin 2. What is this considered?

QUESTION 11

If you have signals leaking from wire to wire in your cabling, it is considered what?

QUESTION 12

A signal naturally weakens over a long distance. This is known as what?

ANSWER 10

A short

ANSWER 11

Crosstalk

ANSWER 12

Attenuation

QUESTION 13

What device can assist with weakening signals due to distance?

QUESTION 14

What can you use to assist with determining bad wiring or bad connectors with network issues?

QUESTION 15

What might you perform before placing APs in a large organization?

ANSWER 13

A repeater

ANSWER 14

A cable tester

ANSWER 15

A site survey

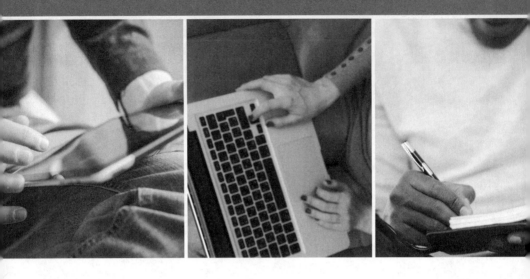

Chapter 21

Other Troubleshooting Areas

QUESTION 1

What issue occurs in a fiber cable if the distance is too far for the signal to work properly?

QUESTION 2

Cable management, such as cable trays, can assist in guarding against what issue with fiber cabling?

QUESTION 3

Your system can communicate with other devices in your VLAN, but it cannot communicate with remote destinations. What might be misconfigured on your device?

ANSWER 1

Attenuation or decibel loss

ANSWER 2

Bend radius limitations

ANSWER 3

The default gateway

QUESTION 4

STP is used to guard against what issue?

QUESTION 5

What can you use to verify end-to-end connectivity, as well as the path that is taken to reach a destination?

QUESTION 6

You notice that your Windows system has an IP address that begins with 169. What is the most likely issue?

ANSWER 4

Layer 2 loops

ANSWER 5

Traceroute

ANSWER 6

You are not communicating with a DHCP server.

QUESTION 7

You suspect that you might have a misconfiguration regarding DNS. What command-line tool can you use to check this?

QUESTION 8

What network management protocol can assist in tracking down issues such as interface errors in your network?

QUESTION 9

What is a standards-based method that enables network devices to discover each other dynamically on the network?

ANSWER 7

nslookup

ANSWER 8

SNMP

ANSWER 9

Link Layer Discovery Protocol (LLDP)

QUESTION 10

An ACL can be used on a firewall to permit or deny traffic. An ACL ends with what entry?

QUESTION 11

What type of network attack seeks to render a service or system unusable, often by flooding traffic at the device?

QUESTION 12

What is often true about ICMP pings and firewalls?

ANSWER 10

The implicit deny all entry

ANSWER 11

Denial of Service (DoS)

ANSWER 12

They are not permitted through the device by default.

QUESTION 13

What should you do before rolling out a major OS update?

QUESTION 14

What routing loop prevention feature might cause an issue with the hub interface in a hub-and-spoke WAN?

QUESTION 15

What protocol did Cisco invent for communicating AAA information from a server to a network device?

ANSWER 13

Test the update in a lab environment first.

ANSWER 14

Split horizon

ANSWER 15

TACACS+

Chapter 22
Networking Standards

QUESTION 1

What is Layer 5 of the OSI model?

QUESTION 2

What is an example of a Layer 3 network device?

QUESTION 3

What is the base-8 numbering system called?

ANSWER 1

The session layer

ANSWER 2

A router

ANSWER 3

Octal

QUESTION 4

What two numbers are used in the binary numbering system?

QUESTION 5

What is the frequency band used by 802.11a?

QUESTION 6

What is the frequency band used by 802.11b?

ANSWER 4

0 and 1

ANSWER 5

5 GHz

ANSWER 6

2.4 GHz

QUESTION 7

What is the frequency band used by 802.11g?

QUESTION 8

What bands can 802.11n use?

QUESTION 9

What is the frequency band used by 802.11ac?

ANSWER 7

2.4 GHz

ANSWER 8

2.4 and 5 GHz

ANSWER 9

5 GHz

QUESTION 10

What is the bandwidth capacity of 100BASE-FX?

QUESTION 11

One end of your cable is terminated using 568A and the other end is 568B. What type of cable is it?

QUESTION 12

Using the T568A standard, what color is used for pin 2?

ANSWER 10

100 Mbps

ANSWER 11

Crossover

ANSWER 12

Green

QUESTION 13

Using the T568B standard, what color is used for pin 5?

QUESTION 14

What system is responsible for manipulating the air consumed by humans?

QUESTION 15

What protocol and port are used by HTTPS?

ANSWER 13

White/blue

ANSWER 14

Heating, ventilation, and air-conditioning (HVAC)

ANSWER 15

TCP 443

QUESTION 16

What protocol and port are used by IMAP?

QUESTION 17

What protocol and port are used by SMTP?

QUESTION 18

What protocol and port are used by SNMP?

ANSWER 16

TCP 143

ANSWER 17

TCP 25

ANSWER 18

UDP 161

QUESTION 19

What protocol and port are used by Telnet?

QUESTION 20

What protocol and port are used by SSH?

QUESTION 21

What protocols and ports are used by DNS?

ANSWER 19

TCP 23

ANSWER 20

TCP 22

ANSWER 21

TCP and UDP, port 53

QUESTION 22

What protocol and ports are used by DHCP?

QUESTION 23

What protocol and port are used by TFTP?

QUESTION 24

What protocol and port are used by SMB?

ANSWER 22

UDP, ports 67 and 68

ANSWER 23

UDP 69

ANSWER 24

TCP 445

QUESTION 25

What protocol and port are used by RDP?

ANSWER 25

TCP 3389

Chapter 1
Network Devices and Services

As today's networks increase in complexity and importance, more and more networking devices and networking services are available. This chapter ensures that you can compare and contrast these various components. Combined with the Flash Cards and practice questions of this text, you can confidently answer the many potential questions regarding these devices and service technologies.

Network Devices

You might encounter more than this list of network devices in your real-world experiences, but this list in the Quick Reference Sheets shows the devices you must know to be successful on the Network+ exam.

Routers—Perhaps one of the most famous of the network devices, the router operates primarily at Layer 3 of the OSI model. This means it must maintain a database of IPv4 and/or IPv6 prefixes that it can reach. This database is termed the routing table. It can be populated automatically, statically, and dynamically using many different available routing protocols. Most routers can perform many other functions, making them a key workhorse of the network. These additional functions include various security mechanisms, Quality of Service (QoS), and Network Address Translation (NAT), just to name a few. The interfaces of routers create separate collision domains as well as separate broadcast domains. Figure 1-1 shows how Cisco likes to represent routers in network diagrams.

Figure 1-1   *A Router as Represented by Cisco Systems*

Switches—Whereas a router possesses just a couple of ports (typically), the switch has many. Some larger enterprise switches have literally hundreds. The switch operates primarily at Layer 2 of the OSI model and, as such, it is largely concerned with MAC addresses. Each port of the switch creates its own collision domain, but by default, each port does not create its own broadcast domain. Whereas routers are obsessed with moving packets between subnets, switches are concerned with switching frames as blindingly fast as possible within the subnet. Figure 1-2 shows how Cisco represents a Layer 2 switch, also termed a *workgroup switch*.

Figure 1-2   *A Switch as Represented by Cisco Systems*

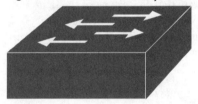

Multilayer Switches—A real beast of a system, the multilayer switch performs the functions of routing and switching in one device. These devices set the speed records when it comes to moving packets as quickly as possible between subnets and within subnets. Figure 1-3 shows a Cisco multilayer switch.

Figure 1-3   *A Multilayer Switch as Represented by Cisco Systems*

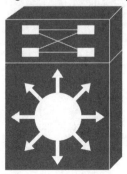

Firewalls—When it comes to securing your network, the firewall is a lead actor. These devices specialize in ensuring that bad people stay out and trusted people are enabled to access the devices and services they need from within the network. Keep in mind that firewalls also come in software varieties, so they are not always a separate physical device. For example, there is a software-based firewall built in to the Windows client operating system. The most popular hardware-based firewalls today are termed *stateful firewalls*. They dynamically permit traffic out of a protected network, and then allow the appropriate return traffic back in. Like routers, firewalls operate on Layer 3 and above of the OSI model. Figure 1-4 shows a firewall as represented by Palo Alto Networks, a very popular maker of firewall software and appliances.

Figure 1-4   *A Firewall as Represented by Palo Alto Networks*

HIDS/HIPS—The Host Intrusion Detection System (HIDS) was one of the first security mechanisms designed for computing devices. Originally intended for the mainframe, its job remains the same today. It examines the packets entering the computer and the processes that are running on the system and alerts users or IT staff regarding activities that are suspicious.

But what if mere detection is not enough? What if you want to prevent the attacks on the host system entirely? HIPS is an installed software package that monitors a single host for suspicious activity by analyzing events occurring within that host and then prevents the attack attempt.

IDS/IPS—Also known as *Network Intrusion Detection Systems* or *Network Intrusion Prevention Systems*, these device seek to alert administrators (detection) about malicious packets attempting to enter the network, or they try to stop (prevention) these packets. There are many styles of IDS and IPS. These include signature-based, in which you load predefined templates that identify bad traffic, and policy-based, which define "normal" traffic for your enterprise. An interesting approach is called a *honey pot*, in which the IDS/IPS device tries to lure attackers by pretending to be an unprotected server system or network device.

Access Point—Access points come in all shapes and sizes. Some are completely wireless, and these usually extend the wireless signal from another access point that is typically connected with a wire to the more traditionally connected network. The access points that connect with one or more wires to the local area network (LAN) are often called *wired access points*. Some access points also include routing capabilities in addition to the switching port. These devices are often called *wireless routers*. Figure 1-5 shows a Cisco wireless access point.

Figure 1-5 *An Access Point as Represented by Cisco Systems*

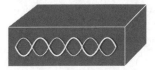

Content Filter—Want to protect your corporate network and keep your employees out of trouble while at work? A content filter seeks to accomplish these goals by blocking the capability to reach certain sites, download specific files, read certain e-mails, or various other controls. Content filtering is accomplished by using a wide variety of software and hardware solutions. For example, many firewalls can also act as content filters in addition to various standalone software packages.

Load Balancer—Another network device that comes in many shapes and sizes is the load balancer. The idea here is software and/or hardware that takes requests and distributes them across many identical resources. Perhaps you have a key database that needs to be checked frequently. You can replicate identical copies of this database, and then have a load balance distribute the requests among these multiple copies. There are many instances in which load balancing is very useful in an IT organization.

Hub—Hubs in the LAN have become legacy devices, being replaced by the faster and more efficient switches. A hub is a Layer 1 device, taking in bits, perhaps trying to strengthen their signal, and then sending these bits out all remaining ports on the device. When traffic is not filtered properly by using Layer 2 addressing, hubs create a large collision domain as well as a single broadcast domain. This large single collision domain increases network collisions. Figure 1-6 shows Cisco's preferred method for representing hubs.

Figure 1-6 *A Hub as Represented by Cisco Systems*

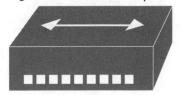

Analog Modem—Another device that is becoming more legacy is the analog modem. It connects to the public switched telephone network (PSTN) to communicate digital signals from the computer over long distances. This technology is slower and less reliable compared to more modern techniques. It is amazing to think that this technology was the main method of accessing the Internet at one time.

Packet Shaper—Whereas a firewall seeks to stop certain forms of traffic from entering your private network, the packet shaper attempts to control the amount of traffic that is permitted. Packet shapers try to enforce your limits on the volume of traffic based on various parameters. Perhaps you want voice and video traffic to have preference over web pages and e-mail. The packet shaping devices can help enforce this policy.

VPN Concentrator—The virtual private network (VPN) has exploded in popularity with increased Internet speeds. The VPN concentrator is typically a hardware device that simultaneously connects as many VPN users as possible. These devices are often located at a corporate headquarters, where many users and branch offices usually make the VPN connection.

Network Services and Applications

Services and applications used for networking purposes are just as important as devices. This section quickly references these for you.

VPNs—The virtual private network seeks to make network users believe they are connected to a system or another network directly, even though this connection might be made across the globe. The public Internet often serves as the connection medium. Strong network security is typically used to keep the transfer of information truly "private." VPNs include the following:

- Site to site—This provides convenience and cost-effectiveness for a branch-office type of environment. One device, such as a router, makes a VPN connection to another site. Then all of the end systems at the local site can connect over the VPN using the router's connection. This eliminates the responsibility for each client system to obtain the appropriate VPN software and its proper configuration.

- Host to site—If a client system installs software to connect to a remote site over a VPN, this is called a *host to site connection*.

- Host to host—As you might guess, in a host to host connection two clients install appropriate software to make a VPN connection with each other. Note that this might be a client and a server operating system as well. The main difference is that there is not an entire site (network) participating in the connection.

Protocols—There are various protocols and configuration options for VPNs today. This is due to their extreme explosion in popularity, and a consistent drive to improve their security and reliability. The following are some protocols you need to be familiar with:

- IPsec—IP Security (IPsec) is a suite of protocols that provides a wide variety of security protections to a VPN. For example, in lower-security environments, IPsec can feature Message Digest Authentication (MD5) for authentication and Data Encryption Standard (DES) for encryption. In a higher-security environment, Secure Hash Algorithm (SHA-1) can be used along with the Advanced Encryption Standard (AES). Tunnel mode can protect the entire packet, or transport mode can focus on protecting just the payload. IPsec support was optional in IPv4, but in IPv6, the node must support IPsec.

- GRE—Generic Routing Encapsulation can be a real workhorse in your network. It is useful in a wide variety of circumstances. One example is if you have traffic that cannot be protected by IPsec. First encapsulate the traffic in GRE, and then compress the GRE traffic within IPsec. It is important to note that GRE by itself does not provide security mechanisms.

- **SSL VPN**—The Secure Sockets Layer VPN enables you to create a VPN connection using your standard web browser as the client software.

- **PTP/PPTP**—The Point-to-Point Tunneling Protocol (PPTP) uses a control channel over TCP and a GRE tunnel operating to encapsulate PPP packets. The PPTP specification does not describe encryption or authentication features and relies on the Point-to-Point Protocol being tunneled to implement security functionality. However, the most common PPTP implementation shipping with the Microsoft Windows product families allows for various levels of authentication and encryption natively as standard features of the Windows PPTP stack.

TACACS/RADIUS—In today's corporate networks there are many devices for which users need to log in. TACACS and RADIUS are security protocols that communicate from a network device to a database of user and group accounts. Often, TACACS and RADIUS are used in a AAA environment. AAA provides accounting, authentication, and authorization services. TACACS is often considered more secure than RADIUS because it protects the entire packet and not just the password as RADIUS does.

RAS—Remote Access Services enable a client to access a server system over a network as vast as the Internet.

Web Services—Many devices today provide HTTP and HTTPS services so that web pages can be accessed from the device. For example, a Cisco router might run the HTTPS service so that administrators can access a web page hosted on the router that provides configuration options for the device.

Unified Voice Services—For years, only data was sent through the network. Now, more voice traffic finds its way on the data network as well. Various devices help make this possible, from sophisticated software packages that replace the traditional PBX system, to digital phones with which end users place calls. Figure 1-7 shows a Cisco representation of an IP phone.

Figure 1-7   *A Voice over IP Phone as Represented by Cisco Systems*

Network Controllers—Network controllers exist on network interface cards (NICs) and permit various types of network devices to connect to the network. On many devices, such as personal computers, the network controller is modular and can easily be swapped for another model or type.

Chapter 2

Configuring Network Services

Some services are absolutely critical to the operation of a network. You should be well versed in their purpose and be able to describe the elements of a typical configuration. This section prepares you for this task.

DHCP

The *Dynamic Host Configuration Protocol* (DHCP) dramatically reduces the administrative workload in the assignment of IP address information. Instead of manually (statically) assigning addresses to workstations, you rely on a router or server operating system to "lease" address information to clients.

DHCP operates in a four-step process:

STEP 1 Discover stage

STEP 2 Offer

STEP 3 Request

STEP 4 Acknowledgment

Just think of Dora the Explorer to remember this.

Static Versus Dynamic Addressing—Static address assignment refers to manually inputting all the required IP address information in your client. Dynamic assignment refers to DHCP. Static assignment is typically reserved for server systems as opposed to client devices.

Reservations—An interesting alternative to the static assignment of an address is a DHCP reservation. Using this approach, you configure the address information for a client on the DHCP server and reserve it for a specific device in your environment. A simple way to identify the device is by the unique MAC address of the system. When the MAC address appears to the DHCP server, the IP address information reserved is assigned. Figure 2-1 shows a DHCP reservation being created.

Figure 2-1   *Creating a DHCP Reservation in Windows Server 2012*

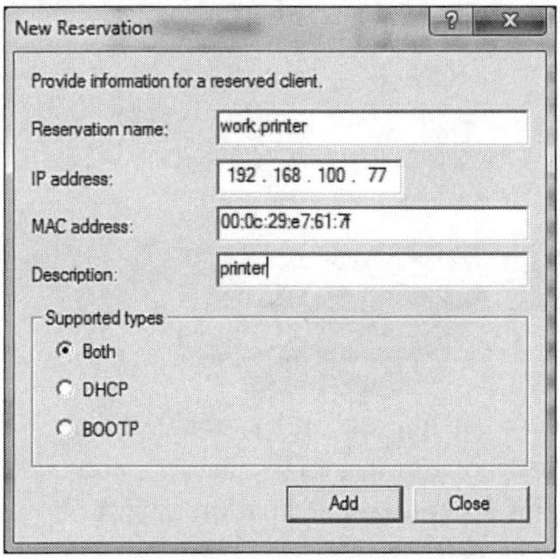

Scopes—The range of address information that you assign to devices using DHCP is called a *scope*. Your DHCP server can consist of many scopes to accommodate various types of networks.

Leases—The actual assignment of configuration information to a client is termed the *lease*. This consists of a specific duration of time before the lease must be renewed or terminated. Figure 2-2 shows scope configuration in a Windows Server.

Figure 2-2   *Scopes and Leases in Windows Server 2012*

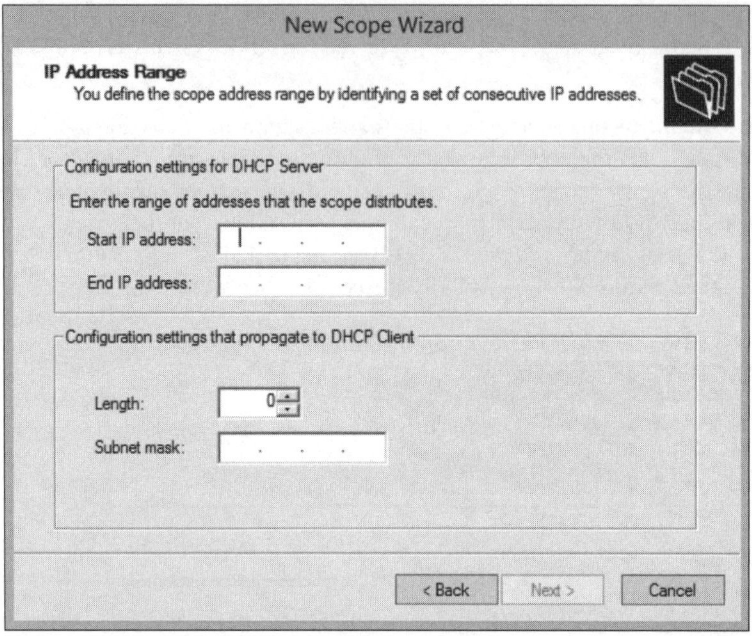

Options—A typical client needs more than just an IP address and a subnet mask. The device requires a default gateway assignment, one or more DNS servers, and many other potential options. You configure this additional information as part of your scope and rely on DHCP for the assignment as well.

IP Helper/DHCP Relay—One issue that looms with DHCP is that a client must broadcast to find a local DHCP server. Naturally, these broadcasts are stopped by routers. A simple router configuration permits you to "relay" these DHCP client broadcasts to a DHCP server in a remote subnet.

DNS

The domain name system (DNS) permits the fast lookup of IP address information for a uniform resource locator (URL) such as www.cbtnuggets.com.

The most common types of records stored in the DNS database include the following:

- A DNS zone's authority (SOA records)
- IP addresses (A and AAAA records)
- SMTP mail exchangers (MX records)
- Name servers (NS records)
- Pointers for reverse DNS lookups (PTR records)
- Domain name aliases (CNAME records)

The domain name system is maintained by a distributed database system that uses the client/server model. The nodes of this database are the name servers. Each domain has at least one authoritative DNS server that publishes information about that domain and the name servers of any domains subordinate to it.

An authoritative name server provides answers that have been configured by an original source, for example, the domain administrator, or by dynamic DNS methods. This is obviously different from a system with answers that were obtained via a regular DNS query to another name server. An authoritative-only name server returns answers to queries about domain names that have been specifically configured by the administrator.

An authoritative name server can be either a master or a slave server. A master server stores the original (master) copies of all zone records. A slave server uses an automatic updating mechanism of the DNS protocol in communication with its master to maintain an identical copy of the master records.

A set of authoritative name servers must be assigned for every DNS zone. An NS record regarding the addresses of that set must be stored in the parent zone and servers themselves. Figure 2-3 shows the DNS configuration interface in Windows Server 2012.

Figure 2-3 *Configuring DNS in Windows Server 2012*

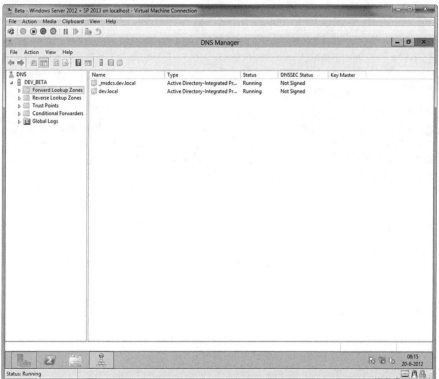

Proxy/Reverse Proxy

A proxy (a computer system or an application) acts as an intermediary for requests from clients seeking resources from other servers. A client connects to the proxy server, requesting some resource from a different server, and the proxy server evaluates the request as a way to simplify and control its complexity. Proxies were invented to add structure and encapsulation to distributed systems. Today, most proxies are web proxies, facilitating access to content on the World Wide Web and providing anonymity.

A *reverse proxy* is a proxy server that appears to clients to be an ordinary server. Requests are forwarded to one or more proxy servers, which handle the request. The response from the proxy server is returned as if it came directly from the origin server, leaving the client no knowledge of the origin server.

NAT

Network Address Translation (NAT) is partially responsible for the significant growth of the Internet. You can use a router to perform translation for many internal, private IP addresses so that these systems can communicate on the public Internet. NAT also comes in handy if your network merges with another that is using the same IP address space!

The simplest type of NAT provides a one-to-one translation of IP addresses; it is often also called a *one-to-one NAT*. Basic NATs can be used to interconnect two IP networks that have incompatible addressing. You can configure the basic NAT one-to-one addressing to occur dynamically by using pools of addresses for translation, or you can configure the translations to occur statically.

The majority of NAT today maps multiple private hosts to one publicly exposed IP address. How can multiple internal clients use the same public IP address? Unique port numbers are used. This is often termed *Port Address Translation* (PAT). For example, you might have one internal host at 10.10.10.10 mapped to 17.13.24.100:2222 and another internal host at 10.10.10.11 mapped to 17.13.24.100:2233.

Port Forwarding

What if you want to host a public web server in your private network? Use port forwarding to accomplish this task. Configure your router to forward HTTP requests to its public IP address to the appropriate IP address and port inside your network. Figure 2-4 shows a typical port forwarding configuration screen on a home wireless router.

Figure 2-4   *The Port Forwarding Configuration Screen of a Typical Wireless Router*

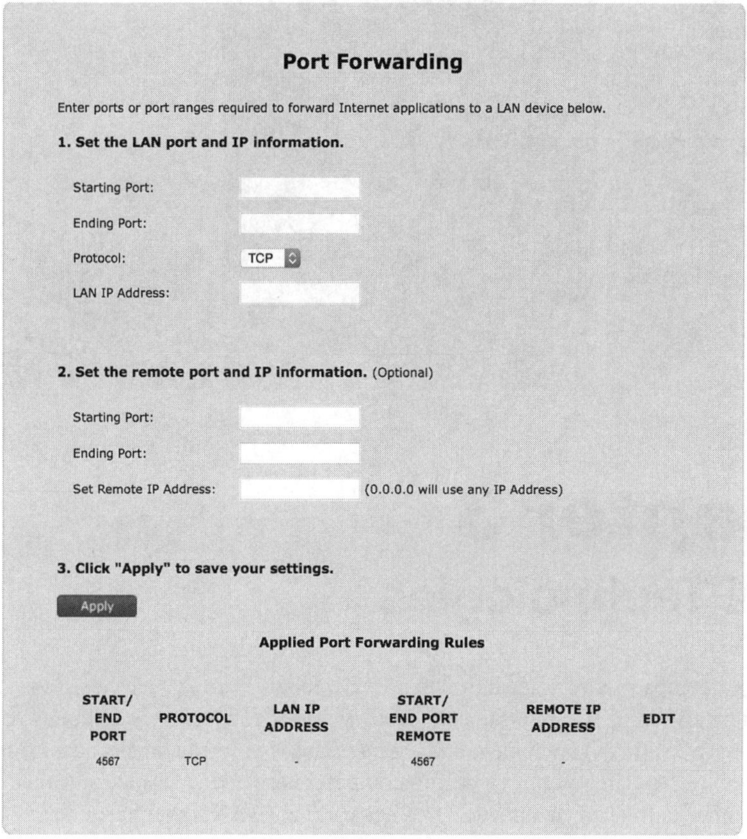

Chapter 3
WAN Technologies

Even if your company is very small, it will not take long before you have employees or branch offices that cannot be connected with fast and relatively inexpensive local area network (LAN) equipment and cabling. This is unfortunate, because "fast and inexpensive" are great terms to hear in computer networking. Thankfully, there have been many advancements in wide area networking (WAN) that make it more tolerable and affordable. Whenever you hear WAN, think about distances beyond the floor of your office building. You might even want to think of the global Internet itself, and don't forget about those satellites beaming signals from space!

Fiber

WAN connections that require a high bandwidth capacity or the capability to span a large distance might use fiber-optic cabling. In addition to the massively long distances that are supported, fiber-optic cabling provides great immunity from electromagnetic interference (EMI).

Synchronous Optical Network (SONET) is a Layer 1 technology that uses fiber-optic cabling as its media. Because SONET is a Layer 1 technology, it can be used to transport various Layer 2 encapsulation types, such as Asynchronous Transfer Mode (ATM). And because SONET uses fiber-optic cabling, it offers high data rates, typically in the 155 Mbps to 10 Gbps range, and long-distance limitations, typically in the 20 km to 250 km range. Optical carrier transmission rates, such as

OC3 (close to 155 Mbps) and OC12 (close to 622 Mbps) are examples of specifica-tions for digital signal transmission bandwidth.

The term *SONET* is often used synonymously with the term *Synchronous Digital Hierarchy* (SDH), which is another fiber-optic multiplexing standard. Although these standards are similar, SONET is typically utilized in North America, whereas SDH has greater worldwide popularity.

A SONET network can vary in its physical topology. For example, devices can con-nect as many as 16 devices in a linear fashion (similar to a bus topology) or in a ring topology. A metropolitan-area network (MAN) often uses a ring topology. The ring might circumnavigate a large metropolitan area. Sites within that metropolitan area could then connect to the nearest point on the SONET ring.

A SONET network uses a single wavelength of light, along with time-division multi-plexing (TDM) to support multiple data flows on a single fiber. This approach differs from dense wavelength division multiplexing (DWDM), which is another high-speed optical network commonly used in MANs. DWDM uses as many as 32 light wave-lengths on a single fiber, and each wavelength can support as many as 160 simultane-ous transmissions using more than eight active wavelengths per fiber. *Coarse wave-length division multiplexing* (CWDM) uses fewer than eight active wavelengths per fiber. Current standards make even more transmissions possible.

Frame Relay

Frame Relay is beginning to decline but is still worthy of inclusion here, especially when you consider regions of the globe outside the United States.

Frame Relay sites are interconnected using virtual circuits (VC). So a single router interface can have multiple VCs. Frame Relay is a Layer 2 technology, and a router uses locally significant identifiers for each VC. These identifiers are called *data-link connection identifiers* (DLCI). Because DLCIs are locally significant, DLCIs at the different ends of a VC do not need to match (although they could).

If a VC is always connected, it is considered to be a *permanent virtual circuit* (PVC). However, some VCs can be brought up on an as-needed basis, and they are referred to as *switched virtual circuits* (SVC).

Unlike a dedicated leased line, Frame Relay shares a service provider's bandwidth with other customers of its service provider. Therefore, subscribers might purchase an SLA (previously described) to guarantee a minimum level of service. In SLA terms, a minimum bandwidth guarantee is called a *committed information rate* (CIR).

During times of congestion, a service provider might need a sender to reduce his transmission rate to the CIR. A service provider can ask a sender to reduce his rate by setting the *backward explicit congestion notification* (BECN) bit in the Frame Relay header of a frame destined for the sender that needs to slow down. If the sender is configured to respond to BECN bits, it can reduce its transmission rate by as much as 25 percent per timing interval (which is 125 ms by default). CIR and

BECN configurations are both considered elements of *Frame Relay Traffic Shaping* (FRTS). A device that does packet shaping is referred to as a *packet shaper*.

Another bit to be aware of in a Frame Relay header is the discard eligible (DE) bit. Recall that a CIR is a minimum bandwidth guarantee for a service provider's customer. However, if the service is not congested, a customer might be able to temporarily transmit at a higher rate. However, frames sent in excess of the CIR have the DE bit in their header set. Then, if the Frame Relay service provider experiences congestion, it might first drop those frames marked with a DE bit.

Satellite

Some locations do not have WAN connectivity options, such as DSL connections or cable modems, commonly available in urban areas. However, these locations might be able to connect to the Internet or to a remote office, using satellite communications. This occurs when a transmission is bounced off of a satellite, received by a satellite ground station, and then sent to its destination using either another satellite hop or a wired WAN connection.

Broadband Cable

Cable television companies have a well-established and wide-reaching infrastructure for television programming. This infrastructure might contain both coaxial and fiber-optic cabling. Such an infrastructure is called a *hybrid fiber-coax* (HFC) distribution network. These networks can designate specific frequency ranges for upstream and downstream data transmission. The device located in a residence (or a business) that can receive and transmit in those data frequency ranges is known as a *cable modem*.

The frequency ranges typically allocated for upstream and downstream data are 5 MHz to 42 MHz upstream and 50 MHz to 860 MHz downstream.

Although the theoretical maximum upstream/downstream bandwidth limits are greater (and dependent on the HFC distribution network in use), most upstream speeds are limited to 2 Mbps, with downstream speeds limited to 10 Mbps. As HFC distribution networks continue to evolve, greater bandwidth capacities become available.

The frequencies dedicated to data transmission are specified by a Data-Over-Cable Service Interface Specification (DOCSIS) version. Although DOCSIS is an international standard, European countries use their own set of frequency ranges, their own standard known as *Euro-DOCSIS*.

DSL/ADSL

Commonplace in many residential and small-business locations (also known as *small office/home office* or *SOHO* locations), *digital subscriber line* (DSL) is a group of technologies that provide high-speed data transmission over existing telephone wiring. DSL has several variants, which differ in data rates and distance limitations.

Three popular DSL variants are

- Asymmetric DSL (ADSL)

- Symmetric DSL (SDSL)

- Very-high-bit-rate DSL (VDSL)

Asymmetric DSL (ADSL) is popular Internet-access solution for residential locations. Note that ADSL enables an existing analog telephone to share the same line used for data for simultaneous transmission of voice and data. The maximum distance from a DSL modem to a DSL access multiplexer (DSLAM) is 18,000 feet. This limitation stems from a procedure that telephone companies have used for decades to change the impedance of telephone lines. A DSLAM acts as an aggregation point for multiple connections, and it connects via an ATM network back to a service provider's router. The service provider authenticates user credentials, obtained via PPPoE, using an authentication server. Also, the service provider has a DHCP server to distribute IP address information to end-user devices (for example, a PC or a wireless router connected to a DSL modem). The term *asymmetric* in *asymmetric DSL* implies that the upstream and downstream speeds can be different. Typically, downstream speeds are greater than upstream speeds in an ADSL connection. The theoretical maximum downstream speed for an ADSL connection is 8 Mbps, and the maximum upstream speed is 1.544 Mbps (the speed of a T1 circuit).

Whereas ADSL has asymmetric (unequal) upstream and downstream speeds, by definition, SDSL has symmetric (equal) upstream and downstream speeds. Another distinction between ADSL and SDSL is that SDSL does not allow simultaneous voice and data on the same phone line. Therefore, SDSL is less popular in residential installations because an additional phone line is required for data. Also, SDSL connections are usually limited to a maximum distance of 12,000 feet between a DSL modem and its DSLAM.

VDSL boasts a much higher bandwidth capacity than ADSL or SDSL, with a common downstream limit of 52 Mbps and a limit of 12 Mbps for upstream traffic.

VDSL's distance limitation is 4,000 feet of telephone cable between a cable modem and a DSLAM. This constraint might seem too stringent for many potential VDSL subscribers, based on their proximity to their closest telephone central office (CO). However, service providers and telephone companies offering VDSL service often extend their fiber-optic network into their surrounding communities. This enables VDSL gateways to be located in multiple communities. The 4,000-foot limitation then becomes a distance limitation between a DSL modem and the nearest VDSL gateway, thus increasing the number of potential VDSL subscribers.

ISDN

Integrated Services Digital Network (ISDN) is a digital telephony technology that supports multiple 64-kbps channels (known as *bearer channels* [B channels]) on a single connection. ISDN was popular back in the 1980s and was used to connect private branch exchanges (PBX), which are telephone switches owned by and operated by a company, to a central office. ISDN has the capability to carry voice, video, or data over its B channels. ISDN also offers a robust set of signaling protocols: Q.921 for Layer 2 signaling and Q.931 for Layer 3 signaling. These signaling protocols run on a separate channel in an ISDN circuit (known as the *delta channel*, *data channel*, or *D channel*).

A *PRI circuit* is an ISDN circuit built on a T1 or E1 circuit. Recall that a T1 circuit has 24 channels. Therefore, if a PRI circuit is built on a T1 circuit, the ISDN PRI circuit has 23 B channels and one 64-kbps D channel. The 24th channel in the T1 circuit is used as the ISDN D channel (the channel used to carry the Q.921 and Q.931 signaling protocols, which are used to set up, maintain, and tear down connections).

Also, recall that an E1 circuit has 32 channels, with the first channel being reserved for framing and synchronization and the seventeenth channel used for signaling. Therefore, an ISDN PRI circuit built on an E1 circuit has 30 B channels and one D channel, which is the seventeenth channel.

Some ISDN circuits are four-wire circuits and some are two-wire. Also, some devices in an ISDN network might not natively be ISDN devices, or they might need to connect to a four-wire ISDN circuit or a two-wire ISDN circuit.

ATM

Asynchronous Transfer Mode (ATM) is a Layer 2 WAN technology that operates using the concept of PVCs and SVCs. However, ATM uses fixed-length cells as its protocol data unit (PDU), as opposed to the variable frames used by Frame Relay. An ATM cell contains a 48-byte payload and a 5-byte header.

An ATM cell's 48-byte payload size resulted from a compromise between the different countries as an international standard for ATM was being developed. Some countries, such as France and Japan, wanted a 32-byte payload size because smaller payload sizes worked well for voice transmission. However, other countries, including the United States, requested a 64-byte payload size because they felt such a size would better support the transmission of both voice and data. In the end, the compromise was to use the average of 32 bytes and 64 bytes (that is, 48 bytes).

Although ATM uses VCs to send voice, data, and video, those VCs are not identified with DLCIs. Instead, ATM uses a pair of numbers to identify a VC. One of the numbers represents the identifier of an ATM virtual path. A single virtual path can contain multiple virtual circuits.

A virtual path is labeled with a virtual path identifier (VPI), and a virtual circuit is labeled with a virtual circuit identifier (VCI). Therefore, an ATM VC can be identified with a VPI/VCI pair of numbers. For example, 100/110 can be used to represent a VC with a VPI of 100 and a VCI of 110.

Interconnections between ATM switches and ATM endpoints are called *user-network interfaces* (UNI), and interconnections between ATM switches are called *network-node interfaces* (NNI).

PPP/Multilink PPP

A common Layer 2 protocol used on dedicated leased lines is *Point-to-Point Protocol* (PPP). PPP has the capability to simultaneously transmit multiple Layer 3 protocols (for example, IP and IPX) through the use of control protocols (CP). IP, as an example, uses the IP control protocol (IPCP).

Each Layer 3 CP runs an instance of PPP's Link Control Protocol (LCP). Four primary features offered by LCP include the following:

- **Multilink interface**—PPP's multilink interface feature enables multiple physical connections to be bonded together into a logical interface. This logical interface allows load balancing across multiple physical interfaces. This is referred to as *Multilink PPP*.

- **Looped link detection**—A Layer 2 loop (of PPP links) can be detected and prevented.

- **Error detection**—Frames containing errors can be detected and discarded by PPP.

- **Authentication**—A device at one end of a PPP link can authenticate the device at the other end of the link. Three approaches to perform PPP authentication are as follows:

  - **Password Authentication Protocol (PAP)**—PAP performs one-way authentication (a client authenticates with a server). A significant drawback to PPP, other than its unidirectional authentication, is the security vulnerability of its clear text transmission of credentials, which could permit an eavesdropper to learn the authentication credentials being used.

  - **Challenge-Handshake Authentication Protocol (CHAP)**—Like PAP, CHAP performs a one-way authentication. However, authentication is performed through a three-way handshake (challenge, response, and acceptance messages) between a server and a client. The three-way handshake enables a client to be authenticated without sending credential information across a network.

  - **Microsoft Challenge-Handshake Authentication Protocol (MS-CHAP)**—MS-CHAP is a Microsoft-enhanced version of CHAP that offers a collection of additional features, including two-way authentication.

MPLS

Multiprotocol Label Switching (MPLS) is growing in popularity as a WAN technology used by service providers. This is due in part to MPLS's capability to support multiple protocols on the same network. MPLS also has the capability to perform traffic engineering (which allows traffic to be dynamically routed within an MPLS cloud based on current load conditions of specific links and availability of alternative paths).

MPLS inserts a 32-bit header between Layer 2 and Layer 3 headers. Because this header is shimmed between the Layer 2 and Layer 3 headers, it is sometimes referred to as a *shim header*. Also, because the MPLS header resides between the Layer 2 and Layer 3 headers, MPLS is considered to be a Layer 2 1/2 technology.

The 32-bit header contains a 20-bit label. This label is used to make forwarding decisions within an MPLS cloud. Therefore, the process of routing MPLS frames through an MPLS cloud is commonly referred to as *label switching*.

An MPLS frame does not maintain the same label throughout the MPLS cloud. Instead, an LSR receives a frame, examines the label on the frame, makes a forwarding decision based on the label, places a new label on the frame, and forwards the frame to the next LSR. This process of label switching is more efficient than routing based on Layer 3 IP addresses. The customer using a provider's network and the MPLS transport across that network is not normally aware of the details of the exact MPLS forwarding that is done by the service provider.

GSM/CDMA

Some cellular-phone technologies (for example, Long-Term Evolution [LTE], which supports a 100-Mbps data rate to mobile devices and a 1-Gbps data rate for stationary devices) can be used to connect a mobile device (such as a smartphone) to the Internet. Other technologies for cellular phones include the older 2G EDGE, which provides slow data rates. EDGE stands for Enhanced Data Rates for GSM Evolution. 2G EDGE was improved upon with 3G, as well as the newer 4G, LTE, and Evolved High-Speed Packet Access (HSPA+). The term *tethering* is commonly used with today's smartphones. Tethering enables a smartphone's data connection to be used by another device, such as a laptop. Also, mobile hotspots are growing in popularity, because these devices connect to a cellphone company's data network. It makes that data network available to nearby devices (typically, a maximum of five devices) via wireless networking technologies. This, for example, enables multiple passengers in a car to share a mobile hotspot and have Internet connectivity from their laptops when riding down the road. Code Division Multiple Access (CDMA) and Global System for Mobiles (GSM) are the two major radio systems used in cellphones.

Dialup

Dialup Internet access uses the facilities of the public switched telephone network (PSTN) to establish a connection to an Internet service provider (ISP) by dialing a telephone number on a conventional telephone line. The user's computer or router uses an attached modem to encode and decode link layer frames and control information into and from audio frequency signals, respectively. Software of the computer encapsulates or extracts Internet protocol packets from the data stream. Despite the proliferation of high-speed Internet access (broadband), dialup Internet access can be used where other forms are not available, such as in rural or remote areas.

WiMAX

Worldwide Interoperability for Microwave Access (WiMAX) provides wireless broadband access to fixed locations (as an alternative to technologies such as DSL) and mobile devices. Depending on the WiMAX service provider, WiMAX coverage areas could encompass entire cities or small countries.

Metro-Ethernet

Ethernet ports (using an RJ-45 connector) are very common and less expensive than specialized serial ports and associated cables. Service providers can offer an Ethernet interface to their customers for their WAN connectivity. The service provider configures the logical connections (in the provider network) required to connect the customer to sites. The technology used in the provider's network is hidden from the customer, allowing what appears to be Ethernet connectivity to each of the customer sites. Actual throughput between sites is controlled by the provider based on the level of service purchased by the customer. Metro-Ethernet is certainly exciting when you consider the speeds possible and the use of such a familiar technology!

Leased Lines

A dedicated *leased line* is typically a point-to-point link interconnecting two sites. All the bandwidth on that dedicated leased line is available to those sites. This means that, unlike a packet-switched connection, the bandwidth of a dedicated leased line connection does not need to be shared among multiple service provider customers.

WAN technologies commonly used with dedicated leased lines include digital circuits, such as T1, E1, T3, and E3 circuits. These circuits use multiplexing technology to simultaneously carry multiple conversations in different 64-kbps channels. A single 64-kbps channel is called a *Digital Signal 0* (DS0).

When one of these circuits comes into your location, it terminates on a device called a *channel service unit/data service unit* (CSU/DSU). Also, be aware that a customary Layer 2 protocol used on dedicated leased lines is PPP. A common connection type used to join to a CSU/DSU is an RJ-48C, which looks similar to an RJ-45(Ethernet) connector. Figure 3-1 shows a dedicated leased line.

Figure 3-1   *A Dedicated Leased Line*

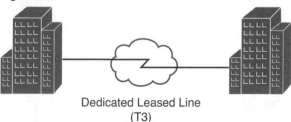

Dedicated Leased Line
(T3)

T1—T1 circuits were originally used in telephony networks, with the intent of one voice conversation being carried in a single channel (that is, a single DS0). A T1 circuit is composed of 24 DS0s, which is called a *Digital Signal 1* (DS1). The bandwidth of a T1 circuit is 1.544 Mbps.

T1 circuits are popular in North America and Japan.

E1—An E1 circuit contains 32 channels, in contrast to the 24 channels on a T1 circuit. Only 30 of those 32 channels, however, can transmit data (or voice or video). Specifically, the first of those 32 channels is reserved for framing and synchronization, and the seventeenth channel is used for signaling (that is, setting up, maintaining, and tearing down a call).

Because an E1 circuit has more DS0s than a T1, it has a higher bandwidth capacity. Specifically, an E1 has a bandwidth capacity of 2.048 Mbps.

Unlike a T1 circuit, an E1 circuit does not group frames together in an SF or ESF. Instead, an E1 circuit groups 16 frames together in a *multiframe*.

E1 circuits are popular outside North America and Japan.

T3—In the same T-carrier family of standards as a T1, a T3 circuit offers an increased bandwidth capacity. Although a T1 circuit combines 24 DS0s into a single physical connection to offer 1.544 Mbps of bandwidth, a T3 circuit combines 672 DS0s into a single physical connection, which is called a *Digital Signal 3* (DS3). A T3 circuit has a bandwidth capacity of 44.7 Mbps.

E3—Just as a T3 circuit provides more bandwidth than a T1 circuit, an E3 circuit's available bandwidth of 34.4 Mbps is significantly more than the 2.048 Mbps of bandwidth offered by an E1 circuit. A common misconception is that the bandwidth of an E3 is greater than the bandwidth of a T3 because an E1's bandwidth is greater than a T1's bandwidth. However, that is not the case—a T3 has a greater bandwidth (that is, 44.7 Mbps) than an E3 (that is, 34.4 Mbps).

CSU/DSU—Although far less popular than they once were, analog modems allowed a phone line to come into a home or business and terminate on analog modems, which provided data connections for devices such as PCs. These analog modems supported a single data conversation per modem.

However, digital circuits (for example, T1, E1, T3, or E3 circuits) usually have multiple data conversations multiplexed together on a single physical connection. Therefore CSU/DSU, a digital modem, is needed, as opposed to an analog modem. This digital modem must be able to distinguish between data arriving on various DS0s.

A CSU/DSU circuit can terminate an incoming digital circuit from a service provider and send properly formatted bits to a router. A CSU/DSU uses clocking (often provided by the service provider) to determine when one bit stops and another starts. Therefore, the circuit coming from a service provider and terminating on a CSU/DSU is a *synchronous circuit* (in which the synchronization is made possible by clocking).

Circuit Switched Versus Packet Switched

A *circuit-switched* connection is brought up on an as-needed basis. In fact, a circuit-switched connection is analogous to a phone call, for which you pick up your phone, dial a number, and a connection is established based on the number you dial. As discussed earlier in this chapter, Integrated Services Digital Network (ISDN) can operate as a circuit-switched connection, bringing up a virtual circuit on demand. This approach to on-demand bandwidth can be a cost savings for some customers who need only periodic connectivity to a remote site.

A *packet-switched* connection is similar to a dedicated leased line because most packet-switched networks are always on. However, unlike a dedicated leased line, packet-switched connections enable multiple customers to share a service provider's bandwidth.

Chapter 4
Install Cables and Connectors

Not everything is wireless these days. It is important to learn the various cable media options as well as the connectors that help make them valuable.

Copper Cables

Most of the cabling seen today is still copper-based. Let's review the options in this section.

Shielded Versus Unshielded—Today's most popular LAN media type is twisted-pair cable, in which individually insulated copper strands are intertwined into a twisted-pair cable. Two categories of twisted-pair cable are *shielded twisted pair* (STP) and *unshielded twisted pair* (UTP).

To define industry-standard pinouts and color-coding for twisted-pair cabling, the TIA/EIA-568 standard was developed. The first iteration of the TIA/EIA-568 standard has come to be known as the TIA/EIA-568-A standard, which was released in 1991.

In 2001, an updated standard was released, which became known as TIA/EIA-568-B. The pinout of these two standards is the same. However, the color-coding of the wiring is different.

Shielded Twisted Pair—If the wires in a cable are not twisted or shielded, that cable can act as an antenna, which might receive or transmit EMI. To prevent this type of behavior, the wires (which are individually insulated) can be twisted together in pairs.

If the distance between the twists is less than a quarter of the wavelength of an electromagnetic waveform, the twisted pair of wires will not radiate that wavelength or receive EMI from that wavelength (in theory, if the wires were perfect conductors). However, as frequencies increase, wavelengths decrease.

One option of supporting higher frequencies is to surround a twisted pair in a metallic shielding, similar to the outer conductor in a coaxial cable. This type of cable is referred to as a *shielded twisted-pair* (STP) cable. The outer conductors shield the copper strands from EMI, but this does add to the expense.

Unshielded Twisted Pair—Another way to block EMI from the copper strands making up a twisted-pair cable is to twist the strands more tightly (that is, more twists per centimeter). By wrapping these strands around each other, the wires insulate each other from EMI.

Because UTP is less expensive than STP, it has grown in popularity since the mid-1990s to become the media of choice for most LANs.

Cat 3, Cat 5, Cat 5e, Cat 6, Cat 6a—UTP cable types vary in their data-carrying capacity.

- **Category 3**—Cat 3 cable is commonly used in Ethernet 10BASE-T networks, which carry data at a rate of 10 Mbps (Mbps stands for megabits per second, meaning millions of bits per second). However, Cat 3 cable can carry data at a maximum rate of 16 Mbps, as seen in some token-ring networks.

- **Category 5**—Cat 5 cable is commonly used in Ethernet 100BASE-TX networks, which carry data at a rate of 100 Mbps. However, Cat 5 cable can carry ATM traffic at a rate of 155 Mbps. Most Cat 5 cables consist of four pairs of 24-gauge wires. Each pair is twisted, with a different number of twists per meter.

- **Category 5e**—Cat 5e cable is an updated version of Cat 5 and is commonly used for 1000BASE-T networks, which carry data at a rate of 1 Gbps. Cat 5e cable offers reduced crosstalk, as compared to Cat 5 cable.

- **Category 6**—Like Cat 5e cable, Cat 6 cable is commonly used for 1000BASE-T Ethernet networks. Some Cat 6 cable is made of thicker conductors (for example, 22-gauge or 23-gauge wire), although some Cat 6 cable is made from the same 24-gauge wire used by Cat 5 and Cat 5e. Cat 6 cable has thicker insulation and offers reduced crosstalk, as compared with Cat 5e.

- **Category 6a**—Cat 6a, or augmented Cat 6, supports twice as many frequencies as Cat 6 and can be used for 10GBASE-T networks, which can transmit data at a rate of 10 billion bits per second (10 Gbps).

PVC Versus Plenum—If a twisted-pair cable is to be installed under raised flooring or in an open-air return, fire codes must be considered. For example, imagine that there was a fire in a building. If the outer insulation of a twisted-pair cable caught on fire or started to melt, it could release toxic fumes. If those toxic fumes were released in a location such as an open-air return, they could be spread throughout a building, posing a huge health risk.

To mitigate the concern of pumping poisonous gas throughout a building's heating, ventilation, and air-conditioning (HVAC) system, plenum cabling can be used. Not only is the outer insulator of a plenum twisted-pair cable fire retardant, but some plenum cabling uses a fluorinated ethylene polymer (FEP) or a low-smoke polyvinyl chloride (PVC) to minimize dangerous fumes.

RG-59—RG-59 is typically used for short-distance applications, such as carrying composite video between two nearby devices. This cable type has loss characteristics such that it is not appropriate for long-distance applications. RG-59 cable has a characteristic impedance of 75 ohms.

RG-6—RG-6 is commonly used by local cable companies to connect individual homes to the cable company's distribution network. Like RG-59 cable, RG-6 cable has a characteristic impedance of 75 ohms.

Straight-Through Versus Crossover Versus Rollover—Most UTP cabling used in today's networks is considered to be *straight-through*, meaning that the RJ-45 jacks at each end of a cable have matching pinouts. For example, pin 1 in an RJ-45 jack at one end of a cable uses the same copper conductor as pin 1 in the RJ-45 jack at the other end of a cable.

However, some network devices cannot be interconnected with a straight-through cable. As an example, consider two PCs interconnected with a straight-through cable. Because the network interface cards (NIC) in these PCs use the same pair of wires for transmission and reception, when one PC sends data to the other PC, the receiving PC receives the data on its transmission wires rather than on its reception wires. For such a scenario, you can use a *crossover cable*, which swaps the transmit and receive wire pairs between the two ends of a cable.

A traditional port found in a PC's NIC is called a *media-dependent interface* (MDI). If a straight-through cable connects a PC's MDI port to an Ethernet switch port, the Ethernet switch port needs to swap the transmit pair of wires (the wires connected to pins 1 and 2) with the receive pair of wires (the wires connected to pins 3 and 6).

Therefore, a traditional port found on an Ethernet switch is called a *media-dependent interface crossover* (MDIX), which reverses the transmit and receive pairs. However, if you want to interconnect two switches, in which both switch ports used for the interconnection are MDIX ports, the cable must be a crossover cable.

NOTE   Most modern Ethernet switches have ports that can automatically detect whether they need to act as MDI ports or MDIX ports and make the appropriate adjustments. This eliminates the necessity of using straight-through cables for some Ethernet switch connections and crossover cables for other connections. With this auto-MDIX feature, you can use either straight-through cables or crossover cables.

Another type of cable is the rollover cable, which is used to connect to a console port to manage a device such as a router or switch. The pin mapping for a rollover cable is 1 <-> 8, 2 <-> 7, 3 <-> 6, 4 <-> 5. The end of the cable looks like an RJ-45 eight-pin connector.

Copper Connectors

The cable is not much use unless it can connect to a network object. That is the job of the aptly named connectors as described in the list that follows:

- **RJ-11**—This is a type 11 registered jack (RJ-11) that has the capacity to be a six-pin connector. However, most RJ-11 connectors have only two or four conductors. An RJ-11 connector is found in most home telephone networks. However, most home phones use only two of the six pins.

- **RJ-45**—This is a type 45 registered jack (RJ-45) that is an eight-pin connector found in most Ethernet networks. However, most Ethernet implementations use only four of the eight pins.

- **RJ-48C**—RJ-48C is used for T1 and ISDN termination and local area data channels/subrate digital services. It uses the eight-position modular connector.

  RJ-48C is commonly used for T1 lines and uses pins 1, 2, 4, and 5.

- **DB-9/RS-232**—A nine-pin D-subminiature (DB-9) connector is commonly used as a connector for asynchronous serial communications. One of the more popular uses of a DB-9 connector is to connect the serial port on a computer with an external modem.

- **DB-25**—The 25-pin D-sub connector is occasionally used in recording studios for multichannel analog audio and AES digital audio. It can also be seen on some modems.

  The D-sub connector family is now in decline for general use in the computer industry due to size and cost. The D-sub series of connectors was invented by ITT Cannon, part of ITT Corporation, in 1952. Cannon's part-numbering system uses D as the prefix for the whole series, followed by one of A, B, C, D, or E denoting the shell size, followed by the number of pins or sockets, followed by either P (plug or pins) or S (socket) denoting the gender of the part. Each shell size usually corresponds to a certain number of pins or sockets: A with 15, B with 25, C with 37, D with 50, and E with 9. For example, DB-25 denotes a D-sub with a 25-position shell size and a 25-position contact configuration.

- **UTP Coupler**—This is used to connect two UTP cables back to back.

- **BNC/BNC Coupler**—A Bayonet Neill-Concelman connector (BNC) (also referred to as British Naval Connector in some literature) can be used for various applications, such as a connector in a 10BASE-2 Ethernet network. A BNC coupler could be used to connect two coaxial cables back to back.

- **F-connector**—This is frequently used for cable TV (including cable modem) connections.

- **66 Block**—This was traditionally used in corporate environments for cross-connecting phone system cabling. As 10-Mbps LANs grew in popularity in the late 1980s and early 1990s, these termination blocks were used to cross-connect Cat 3 UTP cabling. The electrical characteristics (specifically, crosstalk) of a 66 block, however, do not support higher-speed LAN technologies, such as 100-Mbps Ethernet networks.

- **110 Block**—Because 66 blocks are subject to too much crosstalk (that is, interference between different pairs of wires) for higher-speed LAN connections, 110 blocks can terminate a cable (for example, a Cat 5 cable) being used for those higher-speed LANs.

Fiber Cables

Copper is not the only game in town when it comes to cabling technology. This section reviews the key points of fiber cables.

Multimode Fiber (MMF)—This type of optical fiber is mostly used for communication over short distances, such as within a building or on a campus. Typical multimode links have data rates of 10 Mbps to 100 Gbps over link lengths of up to 600 meters (2000 feet)—more than sufficient for the majority of premises applications. Multimode fiber-optic cables use two different types of glass. There is an inner strand of glass (a core) surrounded by an outer cladding of glass, similar to the construction of the previously mentioned coaxial cable.

The light injected by a laser (or an LED) enters the core, and the light is prevented from leaving that inner strand and going into the outer cladding of glass. Specifically, the indices of refraction of these two types of glass are so different that if the light attempts to leave the inner strand, it hits the outer cladding and bends back on itself.

Single-Mode Fiber (SMF)—SMF eliminates the issue of multimode delay distortion by having a core with a diameter so small that it permits only one mode (one path) of propagation. With the issue of multimode delay distortion mitigated, SMF typically has longer distance limitations than MMF.

APC Versus UPC—Fiber-optic cables have different types of mechanical connections. The type of connection impacts the quality of the fiber-optic transmission. Listed from basic to better, the options include Physical Contact (PC), Ultra Physical Contact (UPC), and Angled Physical Contact (APC), which refer to the polishing styles of fiber-optic connectors. The different polishes of the fiber-optic connectors result in different performance of the connector. The less back reflection, the better the transmission. The PC back reflection is –40 dB, the UPC back reflection is around –55 dB, and the APC back reflection is about –70 dB.

Fiber Connectors

Just as in the copper world, the fiber cables need to be connected.

ST—A straight tip (ST) connector is sometimes referred to as a *bayonet connector* because of the long tip extending from the connector. These connectors are most commonly used with MMF. An ST connector links to a terminating device by pushing the connector into the terminating equipment and then twisting the connector housing to lock it in place.

SC—Different literature defines an SC connector as subscriber connector, standard connector, or square connector. The SC connector is attached by pushing the connector into the terminating device, and is removed by pulling the connector from the terminating device.

LC—A Lucent connector (LC) attaches to a terminating device by pushing the connector into the terminating device and is removed by pressing the tab on the connector and pulling it out of the terminating device.

MTRJ—The most unique characteristic of a media termination recommended jack (MTRJ) connector is that two fiber strands (a transmit strand and a receive strand) are included in a single connector. An MTRJ connector is attached by pushing the connector into the terminating device and removed by pulling the connector from the terminating device.

FC—This is a fiber-optic connector with a threaded body, designed for use in high-vibration environments. It is usually implemented with both single-mode optical fiber and polarization-maintaining optical fiber. FC connectors are used in datacom, telecommunications, measurement equipment, and single-mode lasers. They are becoming less common, displaced by SC and LC connectors. The FC connector has been standardized in TIA fiber-optic connector standard EIA/TIA-604-4.

The FC connector was originally called a "Field Assembly Connector" by its inventors. The name "FC" is an acronym for "ferrule connector" or "fiber channel."

Fiber Coupler—A fiber-optic coupler is used in optical fiber systems with one or more input fibers and output fibers. Light entering an input fiber can appear at one or more outputs, and its power distribution potentially depends on the wavelength and polarization. Such couplers can be fabricated in different ways, for example, by thermally fusing fibers so that their cores get into intimate contact. If all involved fibers are single-mode (supporting only a single mode per polarization direction for a given wavelength), there are certain physical restrictions on the performance of the coupler. In particular, it is not possible to combine two or more inputs of the same optical frequency into one single-polarization output without significant excess losses. However, such a restriction does not occur for different input wavelengths; there are couplers that can combine two inputs at different wavelengths into one output without exhibiting significant losses. Wavelength-sensitive couplers are used as multiplexers in wavelength-division multiplexing (WDM) telecom systems to combine several input channels with different wavelengths, or to separate channels.

Media Converters

What if you need to go from one media to another? There is a device for that too. You would use a media converter.

Examples include the following:

- Single-mode fiber to Ethernet
- Multimode fiber to Ethernet
- Fiber to coaxial
- Single-mode to multimode fiber

Tools

If your job in IT has you working with media, you will need a lot of tools. They should include the following:

Cable Crimpers—This tool can be used to attach a connector (for example, an RJ-45 connector) to the end of a UTP cable. To accompany a crimper, you might want to purchase a spool of cable (for example, Category 6 UTP cable) and a box of RJ-45 connectors. You are now equipped to make your own Ethernet patch cables. This is probably less expensive than buying preterminated UTP cables and convenient when you need a patch cable of a nonstandard length or a nonstandard pinout on the RJ-45 connectors (for example, a T1 crossover cable). Many crimpers have a built-in wire stripper and wire snip function as well.

Punch-Down Tool—When you are terminating wires on a punch-down block (a 110 block), you insert an insulated wire between two contact blades. These blades cut through the insulation and make electrical contact with the inner wire. As a result, you do not have to strip off the insulation.

However, if you attempt to insert the wire between the two contact blades using a screwdriver, the blades might be damaged to the point where they will not make a good connection. Therefore, you should use a punch-down tool, which is designed to properly insert an insulated wire between the two contact blades without damaging the blades.

Wire Strippers—This is a small hand-held device used to strip the electrical insulation from electric wires.

Snips—Also known as *shears*, they are hand tools used to cut sheet metal and other tough webs. There are two broad categories: tinner's snips, which are similar to common scissors, and compound-action snips, which use a compound leverage handle system to increase the mechanical advantage.

TDR—Imagine that you have been troubleshooting a network cable (either copper or fiber optic) and you determine that there is a break in (or physical damage to) the cable. It can be problematic to identify exactly where the break exists in a long length of cable. Fortunately, you can use a time domain reflectometer (TDR) for copper cabling or an optical time domain reflectometer (OTDR) for fiber-optic cabling to locate the cable fault.

Both light and electricity travel at speeds approaching 300,000,000 meters per second (approximately 186,000 miles per second), although the speeds are a bit slower and vary depending on the medium. A TDR can send an electric signal down a copper cable (or an OTDR, a light meter, which sends light down a fiber-optic cable), and when the electric signal (or light) encounters a cable fault, a portion of the electric signal (or light) reflects back to the source. Based on the speed of electricity, or light, in the medium and on the amount of time required for the reflected electric signal or light to be returned to the source, a TDR or an OTDR can mathematically determine where the cable fault lies.

Cable Certifier—Different UTP categories support various data rates over specific distances. If you are working with existing cable and want to determine its category, or simply want to test the supported frequency range (and therefore data through-put) of a cable, use a cable certifier. Generally, the testing is performed in two phases. The first phase, called the *opens test*, confirms that each of the intended connections is reliable. The second phase, termed the *shorts test*, verifies that there are no unintended connections.

Chapter 5

Network Topologies and Infrastructures

The way in which networks operate can be divided into topologies. Physical topologies describe how the devices are physically connected (this might include wireless connectivity), and logical topologies outline the traffic flow through the network.

Network Topologies

Many network topologies are in use today in various areas of a typical network. This section details the most important ones you should be aware of as a Network+ candidate.

Mesh—Mesh topology is divided into two types: the *full mesh* and the *partial mesh*. The full mesh is great because every node connects to every other node. This gives the highest degrees of reliability and availability. If one link fails, you can easily communicate around this failure by sending traffic on one of the other available paths. This comes at a cost, however. You must maintain and purchase more links depending on the number of nodes you have. The formula for how many links you will have is $n(n - 1) / 2$ where n is the number of nodes.

A nice compromise is the partial mesh. You add links where additional links between devices are required.

Bus—A bus topology typically uses a cable running through the area requiring connectivity. Devices that need to connect to the network then tap into this nearby cable. Early Ethernet networks commonly relied on bus topologies.

A network tap might be in the form of a T-connector (commonly used in older 10BASE-2 networks) or a vampire tap (usually employed in older 10BASE-5 networks).

Ring—In a ring topology, traffic flows in a circular fashion around a closed network loop (a ring). Usually, a ring topology sends data, in a single direction, to each connected device in turn, until the intended destination receives the data. Token-ring networks typically rely on a ring topology, although the ring can be the logical topology, while physically, the topology is a star topology.

Fiber Distributed Data Interface (FDDI) is another variant of a ring-based topology. Most FDDI networks (which, as the name suggests, have fiber optics as the media) use not just one ring but two. These two rings send data in opposite directions, resulting in counter-rotating rings. One benefit of counter-rotating rings is that if a fiber breaks, the stations on each side of the break can interconnect their two rings, resulting in a single ring capable of reaching all stations on the ring.

Star—A star topology has a central point from which all attached devices radiate. In LANs, that centralized device was typically a hub back in the early 1990s. Modern networks, however, usually have a switch located at the center of the star.

The star topology is the most popular physical LAN topology in use today, with an Ethernet switch at the center of the star and unshielded twisted pair (UTP) cable used to connect from the switch ports to clients. Figure 5-1 shows a current star topology.

Figure 5-1 *A Star Topology*

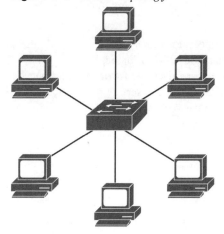

Hybrid—What if you want to achieve the advantages of multiple topologies? Use a hybrid topology. Common examples are star ring networks and star bus networks.

Point-to-Point—When two network devices exclusively connect, it is a point-to-point topology. One advantage is that some processes can be skipped. For example, name resolution is less of an issue because there is only one device on the connection to communicate with.

Point-to-Multipoint—When interconnecting multiple sites (multiple corporate locations) via WAN links, a point-to-multipoint topology is often used. This is also commonly called a *hub-and-spoke* topology. The point-to-multipoint has a WAN link from each remote site (a spoke site) to the main site (the hub site).

With WAN links, a service provider is paid a recurring fee for each link. Therefore, a hub-and-spoke topology helps minimize WAN expenses by not directly connecting any two spoke locations. If two spoke locations need to communicate with each other, their communication is sent via the hub location.

Client-Server—When two devices communicate over a logical topology and one of the devices controls most of the processing work and overhead, this is termed a *client-server* topology. The server does most of the work, which is offloaded from the client device.

Peer-to-Peer—When two devices communicate over the topology and neither device takes on extra workloads or processing, this is termed a *peer-to-peer* arrangement.

Network Infrastructures

To help you describe a network, it is important that you are familiar with the different categories for today's network infrastructures. Note that it might span the globe with a WAN, or be from your wrist to your smart device in your pocket with a PAN.

WAN—A wide area network interconnects network components that are geographically separated. For example, a corporate headquarters might have multiple WAN connections to remote office sites.

MAN—A metropolitan-area network interconnects locations scattered throughout a metropolitan area. Imagine, for example, that a business in Tampa, Florida, had a location near Busch Gardens, another location near Adventure Island, and another location in the Busch Gardens administration buildings. If a service provider could interconnect those locations using a high-speed network, such as a 10-Gbps (that is, 10 billion bits per second) network, the interconnection of those locations would constitute a MAN. One example of a MAN technology is Metro-Ethernet.

LAN—The local area network interconnects network components within a local area (within a building). Examples of common LAN technologies include Ethernet (IEEE 802.3) and wireless networks (IEEE 802.11).

WLAN—If you want to connect your devices wirelessly, and they are in a close proximity to each other such as the same floor of a building, the wireless LAN (WLAN) is an excellent option.

Public places, such as a coffee shop, often provide hotspots for wireless connectivity primarily for Internet access.

PAN—A personal area network has a scale even smaller than that of a LAN. As an example, a connection between a PC and a digital camera via a universal serial bus (USB) cable could be considered a PAN. Another example is a PC connected to an external hard drive via a FireWire connection. A PAN, however, is not necessarily a wired connection. A Bluetooth connection between your cellphone and your car's audio system is considered a wireless PAN (WPAN). The main distinction of a PAN is that its range is typically limited to just a few meters. *Bluetooth*, *infrared* (IR), and *near field communication* (NFC) are examples of technologies that foster a PAN.

SCADA—Supervisory Control and Data Acquisition is a networked computing system operating with coded signals over communication channels that provide control of remote equipment. The control system can be combined with a data acquisition system. This is accomplished by adding the use of coded signals over communication channels to acquire information about the status of the remote equipment for display or for recording functions. SCADA is a type of industrial control system (ICS). Industrial control systems are computer-based systems that monitor and control industrial processes.

Medianets—These are networks that are optimized for high-traffic video. They can detect the type of endpoint device being used. For example, using H.264 AVC (Advanced Video Coding), a medianet can switch to a low-bandwidth video signal when the target is a smartphone rather than a desktop monitor. In addition, it can adjust bandwidth in the same manner when the network is congested. Another advantage of medianets is being able to send IP surveillance video over the same network as corporate data. The proper access controls can be configured for users when the network is aware of the type of device that is sending data.

Chapter 6
Addressing Schemes

It is critical for any engineer to ensure that the addressing used in a network is properly implemented.

IPv6

IPv6 is here. It is important that you review the basics for the Network+ exam.

Address Structure and Address Representation—An IPv6 address has the following address format, where X = a hexadecimal digit in the range of 0–F:

$$XXXX:XXXX:XXXX:XXXX:XXXX:XXXX:XXXX:XXXX$$

A hexadecimal digit is 4 bits in size (4 binary bits can represent 16 values). Notice that an IPv6 address has eight fields, and each field contains four hexadecimal digits. The following formula reveals why an IPv6 address is a 128-bit address:

4 bits per digit × 4 digits per field × 8 fields = 128 bits in an IPv6 address

IPv6 addresses can be difficult to work with because of their size. Fortunately, the following rules exist for abbreviating these addresses:

- Leading 0s in a field can be omitted.

- Contiguous fields containing all 0s can be represented with a double colon.

> **NOTE**   This can be done only once for a single IPv6 address.

Also, the *Extended Unique Identifier* (EUI-64) format can be used to cause a network device to automatically populate the low-order 64 bits of an IPv6 address based on an interface's MAC address.

IPv6 Address Types—IPv6 globally routable unicast addresses start with the first four hex characters in the range of 2000–3999. An IPv6 link local address is also used on each IPv6 interface. The link local address typically begins with FE80. The multicast addresses begin with FF as the first two hex characters. IPv6 can use auto-configuration to discover the current network and select a host ID that is unique on that network. IPv6 can also use a special version of DHCP for IPv6. The protocol that is used to discover the network address and learn the Layer 2 address of neighbors on the same network is *Neighbor Discovery Protocol* (NDP).

IPv6 Data Flows—IPv6 has three types of data flows:

- **Unicast**—With unicast, an IPv6 address is applied to a specific interface. The communication flow can be thought of as a one-to-one communication flow.

- **Multicast**—With multicast, a single IPv6 address (a multicast group) can represent multiple devices on a network. The communication flow is one-to-many.

- **Anycast**—With anycast, a single IPv6 address is assigned to multiple devices. The communication flow is one-to-nearest (from the perspective of a router's routing table).

DHCPv6—The Dynamic Host Configuration Protocol version 6 (DHCPv6) configures Internet Protocol version 6 (IPv6) hosts with IP addresses, IP prefixes, and other configuration data required to operate in an IPv6 network. It is the IPv6 equivalent of the Dynamic Host Configuration Protocol for IPv4.

IPv6 hosts can automatically generate IP addresses internally using stateless address autoconfiguration, or be assigned configuration data with DHCPv6.

IPv6 hosts that use stateless autoconfiguration might require information other than an IP address or route. DHCPv6 can be used to acquire this information, even though it is not being used to configure IP addresses. DHCPv6 is not necessary for configuring hosts with the addresses of domain name system (DNS) servers, because they can be configured using Neighbor Discovery Protocol, which is also the mechanism for stateless autoconfiguration.

Many IPv6 routers, such as those for residential networks, must be configured automatically without operator intervention. Such routers require not only an IPv6 address for use in communicating with upstream routers, but also an IPv6 prefix for use in configuring devices on the downstream side of the router. DHCPv6 prefix delegation provides a mechanism for configuring such routers.

Tunneling—Even if you are designing a network based on IPv4 addressing, a good practice is to consider how readily an IPv6 addressing scheme could be overlaid on that network at some point in the future. Using Teredo tunneling, an IPv6 host could provide IPv6 connectivity even when the host is directly connected to an IPv4-only network. IPv6/IPv4 tunneling is often referred to as *6to4* or *4to6* tunneling, depending on which protocol is being tunneled (IPv4 or IPv6).

IPv4

Address Structure—The binary conversion table is key for working with and understanding 32-bit IP addresses, as shown in Table 6-1.

Table 6-1   *Binary Conversion Table*

2^7	2^6	2^5	2^4	2^3	2^2	2^1	2^0
128	64	32	16	8	4	2	1

An IPv4 address is a 32-bit address. However, rather than writing out each individual bit value, the address is typically written in dotted-decimal notation. Consider the IP address of 10.1.2.3. This address is written in dotted-decimal notation. Notice that the IP address is divided into four individual numbers, separated by periods. Each number represents one-fourth of the IP address. Specifically, each number represents an 8-bit portion of the 32 bits in the address. Because each of these four divisions of an IP address represents 8 bits, these divisions are called *octets*. 00000001 in binary equates to a 1 in decimal. A 00000010 in binary equals 2 in decimal, and 00000011 yields a decimal value of 3.

An IP address is composed of two types of addresses, a network address and a host address. Specifically, a group of contiguous left-justified bits represents the network address, and the remaining bits (a group of contiguous right-justified bits) represent the address of a host on a network. The IP address component that determines which bits refer to the network and which bits refer to the host is called the *subnet mask*. Think of the subnet mask as a dividing line separating an IP address's 32 bits into a group of network bits (on the left) and a group of host bits (on the right).

A subnet mask typically consists of a series of contiguous 1s followed by a set of continuous 0s. In total, a subnet mask contains 32 bits, which correspond to the 32 bits found in an IPv4 address. The 1s in a subnet mask correspond to network bits in an IPv4 address, and 0s in a subnet mask correspond to host bits in an IPv4 address.

Although an IP address (or network address) needs subnet mask information to determine which bits represent the network portion of the address, there are default subnet masks with which you should be familiar. The default subnet mask for a given IP address is solely determined by the value in the IP address's first octet. The default subnet masks are shown in Table 6-2.

Table 6-2   *Default Subnet Masks*

Address Class	Value in First Octet	Classful Mask (Dotted Decimal)	Classful Mask (Prefix Notation)
Class A	1–126	255.0.0.0	/8
Class B	128–191	255.255.0.0	/16
Class C	192–223	255.255.255.0	/24
Class D	224–239	N/A	N/A
Class E	240–255	N/A	N/A

Private Addresses—It is important that you memorize the private-use-only IP addresses listed in Table 6-3.

Table 6-3   *Private Addresses*

Address Class	Address Range	Default Subnet Mask
Class A	10.0.0.0–10.255.255.255	255.0.0.0
Class B	172.16.0.0–172.31.255.255	255.255.0.0
Class B	169.254.0.0–169.254.255.255	255.255.0.0
Class C	192.168.0.0–192.168.255.255	255.255.255.0

APIPA—If a networked device does not have a statically configured IP address and is unable to contact a DHCP server, it still might be able to communicate on an IP network thanks to *Automatic Private IP Addressing* (APIPA). The APIPA feature enables a networked device to self-assign an IP address from the 169.254.0.0/16 network. Note that this address is usable only on the device's local subnet (the IP address is not routable).

Microsoft Windows 8 and 10 default to APIPA if a client is configured to automatically obtain IP address information and that client fails to obtain IP address information from a DHCP server.

MAC Addressing—A media access control address (MAC address) is a unique identifier assigned to network interfaces for communications on the physical network segment. MAC addresses are used as a network address for most IEEE 802 network technologies, including Ethernet and Wi-Fi. Logically, they are used in the media access control protocol sublayer of the OSI reference model.

MAC addresses are often assigned by the manufacturer of a network interface controller (NIC) and are stored in its hardware, such as the card's read-only memory or some other firmware mechanism. If assigned by the manufacturer, a MAC address usually encodes the manufacturer's registered identification number and can be referred to as the *burned-in address* (BIA). It is also known as an *Ethernet hardware address* (EHA), hardware address, or *physical address*. This can be contrasted with a *programmed address*, in which the host device issues commands to the NIC to use an arbitrary address.

A network node can have multiple NICs, and each NIC must have a unique MAC address.

The standard (IEEE 802) format for printing MAC-48 addresses in human-friendly form is six groups of two hexadecimal digits, separated by hyphens (-) or colons (:), in transmission order (for example, 01-23-45-67-89-ab or 01:23:45:67:89:ab). This form is also commonly used for EUI-64. Another convention employed by networking equipment uses three groups of four hexadecimal digits separated by dots (.) (for example, 0123.4567.89ab), again in transmission order.

Subnetting—The way to take a classful network (a network using a classful subnet mask) and divide that network into multiple subnets is by adding 1s to the network's classful subnet mask. However, the class of the IP address does not change, regardless of the new subnet mask. For example, if you took the 172.16.0.0/16 network and subnetted it into multiple networks using a 24-bit subnet mask (172.16.0.0/24, 172.16.1.0/24, 172.16.2.0/24, ...) those networks would still be Class B networks.

Specifically, the class of a network is entirely determined by the value of the first octet. The class of a network has nothing to do with the number of bits in a subnet, making this an often-misunderstood concept.

As another example, the network 10.2.3.0/24 has the subnet mask of a Class C network (a 24-bit subnet mask). However, the 10.2.3.0/24 network is a Class A network, because the value of the first octet is 10. It's simply a Class A network that happens to have a 24-bit subnet mask.

When you add bits to a classful mask, they are referred to as *borrowed bits*. The number of borrowed bits you use determines how many subnets are created and the number of usable hosts per subnet.

To determine the number of subnets created when adding bits to a classful mask, use the following formula:

Number of created subnets = 2^s, where s is the number of borrowed bits

The number of host addresses is calculated as follows:

Number of assignable IP address in a subnet = $2^h - 2$, where h is the number of host bits in the subnet mask

You can calculate what blocks of addresses are used for subnetting. As an example, if you took the 172.25.0.0/16 and subnetted it with a 24-bit subnet mask, the resulting subnets would be as follows:

172.25.0.0/24

172.25.1.0/24

172.25.2.0/24

...

172.25.255.0/24

Notice in the preceding example that you count by 1 in the third octet to calculate the new networks. To determine in what octet you start counting and by what increment you count, a new term needs to be defined. The *interesting octet* is the octet containing the last 1 in the subnet mask.

In this example, the subnet mask was a 24-bit subnet mask, which has a dotted-decimal equivalent of 255.255.255.0 and a binary equivalent of 11111111.11111111.11 111111.00000000. From any of these subnet mask representations, you can determine that the third octet is the octet to contain the last 1 in the subnet mask. Therefore, you are changing the value of the third octet to calculate the new networks.

Now that you realize the third octet is the interesting octet, you need to know by what increment to count in that octet. This increment is known as the *block size*. The block size is calculated by subtracting the subnet mask value in the interesting octet from 256. In this example, the subnet mask had a value of 255 in the interesting octet (the third octet). If you subtract 255 from 256, you get a result of 1 (that is, 256 − 255 = 1). The first subnet is the original network address, with all the borrowed bits set to 0. After this first subnet, start counting by the block size (1, in this example) in the interesting octet to calculate the remainder of the subnets.

The steps for calculating subnets are as follows:

STEP 1   Determine the interesting octet by determining the last octet in the subnet mask to contain a 1.

STEP 2   Determine the block size by subtracting the decimal value in the subnet's interesting octet from 256.

STEP 3   Determine the first subnet by setting all the borrowed bits (which are bits in the subnet mask beyond the bits in the classful subnet mask) to 0.

STEP 4   Determine additional subnets by taking the first subnet and counting by the block size increment in the interesting octet.

Now that you know the subnets created from a classful network given a subnet mask, the next logical step is to determine the usable addresses within those subnets. Recall that you cannot assign an IP address to a device if all the host bits in the IP address are set to 0, because an IP address with all host bits set to 0 is the address of the subnet itself.

Similarly, you cannot assign an IP address to a device if all the host bits in the IP address are set to 1 because an IP address with all host bits set to 1 is the directed broadcast address of a subnet.

CIDR (Classless Inter-Domain Routing)—Although subnetting is the process of extending a classful subnet mask (adding 1s to a classful mask), CIDR does just the opposite. Specifically, CIDR shortens a classful subnet mask by borrowing bits from the network portion of the address. As a result, CIDR enables contiguous classful networks to be aggregated. This process is sometimes called *route aggregation*.

A typical use of CIDR is a service provider summarizing multiple Class C networks, assigned to their various customers. For example, imagine that a service provider is responsible for advertising the following Class C networks:

192.168.32.0/24

192.168.33.0/24

192.168.34.0/24

192.168.35.0/24

The service provider could advertise all four networks with a single route advertisement of 192.168.32.0/22. To calculate this advertisement, convert the values in the third octet. Then, determine how many bits the networks have in common. The number of common bits then becomes the number of bits in the CIDR mask.

Chapter 7

Routing Concepts

Routing information between subnets is a key function of the network. This chapter reviews the elements you need to master.

Loopback Interface—For testing purposes and sourcing packets, loopback interfaces are critical. These virtual interfaces can be added to routers as needed. The practical number is really just a limit on your router resources. The space reserved for loopback interfaces is 127.0.0.0. In IPv6 ::1 is used. Different systems use different specific loopback addresses. 127.0.0.1 is often used.

Routing Loops—Some dynamic routing protocols (like distance vector) are so simple in their operation, they might be prone to a routing loop. This occurs when one router sends traffic to another, just to have that router send the traffic back! Distance-vector routing protocols typically use one of two approaches for preventing routing loops:

- **Split horizon**—This prevents a route learned on one interface from being advertised back out that same interface.

- **Poison reverse**—This causes a route received on one interface to be advertised back out that same interface with a metric considered to be infinite.

Routing Tables—This is a key ingredient of the router—storing the prefixes that the router knows how to reach. The IP routing table is searched by the router for a best match. Best match is determined by the longest prefix match. This is the most specific route to reach a destination.

Static Versus Dynamic Routes—Routing information can be populated in one of three ways:

- The router is directly connected to the subnet.

- The administrator places the route in the table (static).

- The router dynamically learns the prefix information from a dynamic routing protocol.

Default Route—What if your router cannot find a specific match for a prefix? It can send the traffic using a "catch all"—a default route to 0.0.0.0/0 that would match everything else. This is often placed on a device statically by an administrator, so you often see it as default static route. Please note that dynamic routing protocols can inject this route as well, so it does not always have to be static.

Distance Vector—RIPv2—Routing Information Protocol (RIP) is the simplest of all protocols presented in Network+. It uses a very basic metric of hop count. One path is compared against another based on how many router hops it takes to get to the destination. The maximum number of hops between two routers in an RIP-based network is 15. Therefore, a hop count of 16 is considered to be infinite. Also, RIP is an Interior Gateway Protocol (IGP).

Because it is distance vector, RIP version 2 functions by having each device multicast to its neighbors the complete routing table information, even if there have been no changes in the topology. This is known as *routing by rumor* because a device is trusting the routing information provided by a neighbor to route traffic.

Border Gateway Protocol (BGP)—This is the only Exterior Gateway Protocol (EGP) in widespread use today. In fact, BGP is considered to be the routing protocol that runs the Internet, which is an interconnection of multiple autonomous systems. Although some literature classifies BGP as a distance-vector routing protocol, it can more accurately be described as a path-vector routing protocol because it can use as its metric the number of autonomous system (AS) hops that must be transited to reach a destination network, as opposed to a number of required router hops. BGP's path selection is not solely based on AS hops. BGP has various other parameters that it can consider. Interestingly, none of those parameters is based on link speed. Also, although BGP is incredibly scalable, it does not quickly converge in the event of a topological change.

Link-State Routing Protocols—OSPF—This is a link-state routing protocol that uses a metric of cost, which is based on the link speed between two routers. Open Shortest Path First (OSPF) is a popular IGP because of its scalability, fast convergence, and vendor interoperability. It uses the concept of areas, which enables it to be very scalable compared to other IGPs.

IS-IS—This link-state routing protocol is similar in its operation to OSPF. It uses a configurable, yet dimensionless, metric associated with an interface and, like

OSPF, runs Dijkstra's Shortest Path First algorithm. Although Intermediate System–Intermediate System (IS-IS) as an IGP offers the scalability, fast convergence, and vendor-interoperability benefits of OSPF, it has not been as widely deployed as OSPF.

Route Redistribution—What if you merge with another company that is running OSPF and you are running RIP v2? Is there any way to immediately share routing information between your systems without replacing one of the two routing protocols? The answer is yes. Redistribution. A network can simultaneously support more than one routing protocol through the process of route redistribution. For example, a router could have one of its interfaces participating in an OSPF area of the network and have another interface participating in an RIP v2 area. It could then take routes learned via OSPF and inject those routes into the RIP v2 routing process. Similarly, RIP v2–learned routes could be redistributed into the OSPF routing process.

High Availability—End systems not running a routing protocol point to a default gateway. The default gateway is traditionally the IP address of a router on the local subnet. However, if the default gateway router fails, the end systems are unable to leave their subnet.

- **Hot Standby Router Protocol (HSRP):** This is a Cisco proprietary approach to first-hop redundancy.

  Imagine a workstation configured with a default gateway (a next-hop gateway) of 172.16.1.3. To prevent the default gateway from becoming a single point of failure, HSRP enables multiple routers on the subnet to each act as the default gateway, supporting the virtual IP address of the HSRP group (172.16.1.3), although only one of the routers acts as the default gateway at any given time. Under normal conditions, say R1 (the active router) forwards packets sent to virtual IP 172.16.1.3. However, if router R1 is unavailable, router R2 (the standby router) can take over and start forwarding traffic sent to 172.16.1.3. Notice that neither router R1 nor router R2 has a physical interface with an IP address of 172.16.1.3. Instead, a logical router, called a *virtual router*, that is serviced by either router R1 or R2 maintains the 172.16.1.3 IP address.

- **Virtual Router Redundancy Protocol (VRRP):** VRRP is an Internet Engineering Task Force (IETF) open standard that operates in a similar method as the Cisco proprietary HSRP.

With each of these technologies, the MAC address and the IP address of a default gateway can be serviced by more than one router (or multilayer switch). Therefore, if a default gateway becomes unavailable, the other router (or multilayer switch) can take over, still servicing the same MAC and IP addresses.

Administrative Distance—If a network is running more than one routing protocol (maybe as a result of a corporate merger), and a router receives two route advertisements from different routing protocols for the same network, which route advertisement does the router believe? Some routing protocols are considered to be more believable than others. This is based on the sophistication of the routing protocol. For example, because OSPF is so much more complex and sophisticated when compared to RIP v2, it has the lower (better) administrative distance score.

The administrative distance scores for most protocols are shown in Table 7-1.

Table 7-1 *Administrative Distance Scores*

Routing Information Source	Administrative Distance
Directly connected network	0
Statically configured network	1
Enhanced Interior Gateway Protocol (EIGRP)	90
OSPF	110
RIP	120
External EIGRP	170
Unknown or unbelievable	255 (considered to be unreachable)

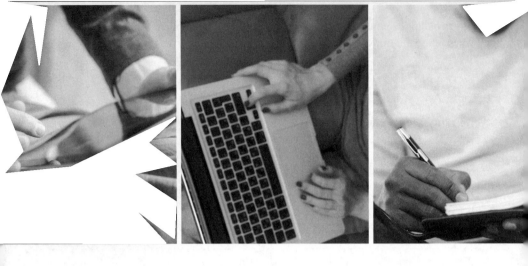

Chapter 8

Unified Communications Technologies

Voice over IP is one of the most exciting areas in IT right now. Why maintain two networks (voice and data) when you can become so much more efficient with one?

Voice over IP Protocols and Components

A voice over IP (VoIP) network digitizes the spoken voice into packets and transmits them across a data network. This enables voice, data, and even video to share the same medium. In a network with unified communications (UC) such as voice, video, and data, specialized UC servers, controllers, devices, and gateways are also likely to be used. In a cloud computing environment, they can be virtualized as well.

Not only can a VoIP network provide significant cost savings over a traditional PBX solution, but many VoIP networks offer enhanced services, such as integration with videoconferencing applications and calendaring software to determine availability, which are not found in traditional corporate telephony environments.

IP Phone—This is a telephone with an integrated Ethernet connection. Although users speak into a traditional analog handset (or headset) on the IP phone, the IP phone digitizes the spoken voice, packetizes it, and sends it out over a data network (via the IP phone's Ethernet port).

Call Agent—This is a repository for a VoIP network's dial plan. For example, when a user dials a number from an IP phone, the call agent analyzes the dialed digits and determines how to route the call toward the destination.

Gateway—Located in a VoIP network, this acts as a translator between two different telephony signaling environments. Figure 8-1 shows a video gateway as represented by Cisco Systems.

Figure 8-1   *Video Gateway*

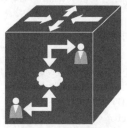

PBX—A private branch exchange (PBX) is a privately owned telephone switch traditionally used in corporate telephony systems. Although a PBX is not considered a VoIP device, it can connect into a VoIP network through a gateway. Figure 8-2 shows a Cisco Call Manager (CCM). This is the modern VoIP replacement for the PBX.

Figure 8-2   *CCM*

Analog Phone—This is a traditional telephone, like you might have in your home. Even though an analog phone is not typically considered a VoIP device, it can connect into a VoIP network via a VoIP or, as shown in Figure 8-2, via a PBX, which is connected to a VoIP network.

SIP—Session Initiation Protocol (SIP) is a VoIP signaling protocol used to set up, maintain, and tear down VoIP phone calls. SIP is spoken between the IP phone and the call agent to establish a call. The call agent then uses SIP to signal a local gateway to route the call. That gateway uses SIP (across an IP WAN) to signal the remote gateway about the incoming call.

RTP—Real-time Transport Protocol (RTP) carries voice and interactive video. A bidirectional RTP stream does not flow through the call agent.

Codec—This is a device or computer program capable of encoding or decoding a digital data stream or signal. A codec encodes a data stream or signal for transmission, storage, or encryption, or decodes it for playback or editing. Codecs are used in videoconferencing, streaming media, and video editing applications. A video camera's analog-to-digital converter (ADC) changes its analog signals into digital signals, which are then passed through a video compressor for digital transmission or storage. A receiving device then runs the signal through a video decompressor, then a digital-to-analog converter (DAC) for analog display.

> **NOTE**   Remember that you need many of these components in your video-based networks as well. Voice and video are nearly interchangeable in this discussion.

QoS Technologies—Quality of Service (QoS) is a suite of technologies that enables you to strategically optimize network performance for select traffic types. For example, in today's converged networks (networks simultaneously transporting voice, video, and data), some applications such as voice might be more intolerant of delay (latency) than other applications. For example, an FTP file transfer is less latency sensitive than a VoIP call. Fortunately, through the use of QoS technologies, you can identify which traffic types need to be sent first, how much bandwidth to allocate to various traffic types, which traffic types should be dropped first in the event of congestion, and how to make the most efficient use of the relatively limited bandwidth of an IP WAN.

A lack of bandwidth is the overshadowing issue for most quality problems. Specifically, packets might suffer from one or more of these symptoms:

- **Delay**—This is the time required for a packet to travel from its source to its destination. You might have witnessed delay on the evening news, when the news anchor is talking via satellite to a foreign news correspondent. Because of the satellite delay, the conversation begins to feel unnatural.

- **Jitter**—This is the uneven arrival of packets. For example, imagine a VoIP conversation in which packet 1 arrives at a destination router. Then, 20 ms later, packet 2 arrives. After another 70 ms, packet 3 arrives, and then packet 4 arrives 20 ms behind packet 3. This variation in arrival times (variable delay) is not dropping packets, but this jitter might be interpreted by the listener as dropped packets.

- **Drops**—Packet drops occur when a link is congested and a router's interface queue overflows. Some types of traffic, such as UDP traffic carrying voice packets, are not retransmitted if packets are dropped.

QoS features are categorized into one of the three categories:

- Best-effort
- Integrated Services
- Differentiated Services

Best-effort treatment of traffic does not truly provide QoS to that traffic, because there is no reordering of packets. It uses a first-in, first-out (FIFO) queuing strategy, in which packets are emptied from a queue in the same order in which they entered it.

Integrated Services (IntServ) is often referred to as *hard QoS* because it can make strict bandwidth reservations. IntServ uses signaling among network devices to provide bandwidth reservations. Resource Reservation Protocol (RSVP) is an example of an IntServ approach to QoS. Because IntServ must be configured on every router along a packet's path, the main drawback of IntServ is its lack of scalability.

Differentiated Services (DiffServ), as its name suggests, distinguishes between multiple traffic flows. Specifically, packets are marked, and routers and switches can then make decisions such as dropping or forwarding decisions based on those markings. Because DiffServ does not make an explicit reservation, it is often called *soft QoS*. Most modern QoS configurations are based on the DiffServ approach. The following is a collection of commonly used QoS mechanisms:

- **Classification**—Placing the different traffic forms in your network in the appropriate QoS category

- **Marking**—Using Differentiated Services Code Point (DSCP) at Layer 3 and Class of Service (CoS) at Layer 2

- **Congestion management**—Using tools to handle congestion when it occurs

- **Congestion avoidance**—Trying to avoid congestion altogether

- **Policing and shaping**—Smoothing out various forms of traffic

- **Link efficiency**—Using tools such as compression and fragmentation to improve a slow link function with important traffic

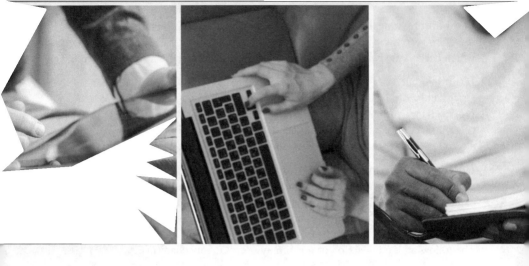

Chapter 9

Cloud and Virtualization

A major data center paradigm shift is underway that eliminates the need for companies to have their own data centers. Multiple physical servers housed in one location that offer specific service such as e-mail, DNS services, or Microsoft Active Directory are no longer a necessity.

Virtual Network Devices

There are so many areas of virtualization, especially with the trend toward virtual devices.

Virtual Servers—This type of server is more prevalent than ever. The computing power available in a single high-end server is often sufficient to handle the tasks of multiple independent servers. With the advent of virtualization, multiple servers (which might be running different operating systems) can run in virtual server instances on one physical device. For example, a single high-end server might be running an instance of a Microsoft Windows Server providing Microsoft Active Directory (AD) services to an enterprise, while simultaneously running an instance of a Linux server acting as a corporate web server, and at the same time acting as a Sun Solaris UNIX server providing corporate DNS services.

Virtual Routers and Firewalls—Most of the vendors who create physical routers and firewalls also offer virtualized ones. The benefit of using a virtualized firewall or router is that the same features of routing and security are available in the virtual environment as in the physical one. As part of interfacing with virtual networks, virtual network adapters are used. For connectivity between the virtual world and the physical one, there are physical interfaces involved that connect to the logical virtual interfaces.

Virtual Switches—One potential trade-off you make with the previously described virtual server scenario is that all servers belong to the same IP subnet, which could have QoS and security implications. If these server instances run on separate physical devices, they can be attached to different ports on an Ethernet switch. These switch ports could belong to different VLANs, which can place each server in a different broadcast domain.

> **NOTE** Some virtual servers enable you to maintain Layer 2 control (VLAN separation and filtering). This Layer 2 control is made possible by the virtual server not only virtualizing instances of servers, but also virtualizing a Layer 2 switch.

Virtual Desktops—Users are more mobile than ever. Access to information traditionally stored on office computers' hard drives from various locations is required. For example, you might be at an airport using your smartphone and need access to a document that you created on your office computer. With virtual desktops your data is stored in a data center rather than on an office computer's hard drive. When authentication credentials are provided, a secure connection can be established between the centralized repository of user data and that device, thus enabling you to remotely access your document.

Additional Virtualization Solutions—Although virtual servers, virtual switches, and virtual desktops were described as residing at a corporate location (on-site), some service providers provide off-site options. Specifically, if you prefer not to house and maintain your own data center, these virtualization technologies can be located at a service provider's data center. You can be billed based on usage patterns. Such a service provider offering is called *Network as a Service* (NaaS), implying that network features are provided by a service provider, just as a telephony service provider offers access to the public switched telephone network (PSTN) and an ISP offers access to the public Internet.

Cloud Computing

Virtualized services and solutions offered by service providers are termed *cloud computing*.

Cloud Types

A company purchasing cloud computing services has four options: public, private, hybrid, or community cloud services.

Public Cloud—This type of cloud offers services over a network that is open for public use. Public cloud services might be free. Technically, there might be little or no difference between public and private cloud architecture. However, security considerations can be substantially different for services (applications, storage, and other resources) that are made available by a service provider for a public audience and when communication is effected over a nontrusted network. Generally, public cloud service providers such as Amazon Web Services (AWS), Microsoft, and Google own and operate the infrastructure at their data centers, and access is generally via the Internet. AWS and Microsoft also offer direct connect services called AWS Direct Connect and Azure ExpressRoute, respectively. Such connections require customers to purchase or lease a private connection to a peering point offered by the cloud provider.

Private Cloud—This is a cloud computing platform implemented within the corporate firewall, under the control of the IT department. A private cloud is designed to offer the same features and benefits of public cloud systems but removes a number of objections to the cloud computing model, including control over enterprise and customer data, worries about security, and issues connected to regulatory compliance.

Hybrid Cloud—This is a composition of two or more clouds (private, community, or public) that remain distinct entities but are bound together, offering the benefits of multiple deployment models. Hybrid cloud can also mean the capability to connect collocation, managed, and/or dedicated services with cloud resources.

Community Cloud—This is a collaborative effort in which infrastructure is shared among several organizations from a specific community with common concerns (security, compliance, jurisdiction, and so on), whether managed internally or by a third party and hosted internally or externally. The costs are spread over fewer users than a public cloud (but more than a private cloud), so only some of the cost-savings potential of cloud computing are realized.

Additional Cloud Services

IaaS (Infrastructure as a Service)—In this type of service the company rents virtualized servers (which are hosted by a service provider) and then runs specific applications on those servers.

SaaS (Software as a Service)—This is another type of cloud service in which the details of the servers are hidden from the customer. The customer's experience is similar to using a web-based application. An application service provider (ASP) provides access to subscribers.

PaaS (Platform as a Service)—This type of cloud service provides a platform for companies that are developing applications and want to focus on creating the software without dealing with the servers and infrastructure that are being used for that development.

Software-Defined Networking—This is changing the landscape of our traditional networks. A well-implemented software-defined network enables the administrator to implement features and functions and configurations without the need for individual command-line configuration on the network devices. The front end that the administrator interfaces with enables him to see what the network is currently doing. Then through that same graphical user interface, the administrator can indicate what he wants accomplished. Behind the scenes, across multiple network devices, the detailed configurations are implemented by the software-defined network.

Storage Area Networking (SAN)—This is the ultimate in storage infrastructures. It creates a dedicated network for the purpose of storing and virtualizing the actual data of the data center.

iSCSI—iSCSI is an acronym for Internet Small Computer System Interface, an Internet protocol (IP)–based storage networking standard for linking data storage facilities. By carrying SCSI commands over IP networks, iSCSI is used to facilitate data transfers over intranets and to manage storage over long distances. iSCSI can be used to transmit data over local area networks (LAN), wide area networks (WAN), or the Internet and can enable location-independent data storage and retrieval.

The protocol permits clients or *initiators* to send SCSI commands (CDBs) to SCSI storage devices (targets) on remote servers. It is a SAN protocol that enables organizations to consolidate storage into data-center storage arrays while providing hosts (such as database and web servers) with the illusion of locally attached disks.

Jumbo Frame—These are Ethernet frames with more than 1500 bytes of payload. Conventionally, jumbo frames can carry up to 9000 bytes of payload, but variations exist and some care must be taken using the term. Many Gigabit Ethernet switches and Gigabit Ethernet network interface cards support jumbo frames. Some Fast Ethernet switches and Fast Ethernet network interface cards also support jumbo frames, but most commercial Internet service providers do not.

Fibre Channel—Fibre Channel (FC) is a high-speed network technology (commonly running at 2-, 4-, 8-, and 16-gigabit-per-second rates) primarily used to connect computer data storage. It is standardized in the T11 Technical Committee of the International Committee for Information Technology Standards (INCITS), an American National Standards Institute (ANSI)–accredited standards committee. Fibre Channel was primarily used in supercomputers but has become a common connection type for SANs in enterprise storage. Despite its name, Fibre Channel signaling can run on an electrical interface in addition to fiber-optic cables.

Fibre Channel Protocol (FCP) is a transport protocol (similar to TCP used in IP networks) that predominantly transports SCSI commands over Fibre Channel networks.

Network Attached Storage—An alternative to the SAN, network attached storage (NAS) is a file-level computer data storage server connected to a computer network that provides data access to a heterogeneous group of clients. NAS not only operates as a file server, but is specialized for this task by its hardware, its software, or a configuration of those elements. NAS is often manufactured as a computer appliance—a specialized computer built from the ground up for storing and serving files—rather than simply a general-purpose computer being used for the role.

Chapter 10

Implement a Basic Network

If you are tasked with implementing the network in your enterprise, you must be aware of many potential considerations that could impact the overall success of your project. This chapter reviews key items to consider, from assessing the network requirements to crucial security issues.

List of Requirements—In addition to basic things such as routing, WAN, and security services, you must consider budget planning for the following benefits to provide for a more efficient organization:

- Functionality—How well does your network meet the needs of the business?

- Scalability—How easy is it to grow your network?

- Availability—How often are the network services available?

- Performance—How well does the equipment perform when it is available?

- Manageability—How easy is it to detect faults and keep the network running smoothly?

- Efficiency—Are the operational costs of the network reasonable and affordable?

Remember, it is rare that you get to implement the network in a vacuum. Often, you must follow these critical steps:

STEP 1   Identify the customer network requirements.

STEP 2   Characterize the existing network.

STEP 3   Design the network topology and solutions proposed.

Device Types/Requirements—Often, the exact devices you purchase for the network are driven by business forces, potentially including these:

- **Return on investment (ROI)**—Whether it is a great cost savings, or increased productivity, or both, businesses expect a nice ROI based on the network you build. Even if it is a home network for yourself, you want to see an adequate ROI.

- **Regulations**—Often, your choices of devices include meeting the requirements of industry or corporate regulations. For example, the Health Insurance Portability and Accountability Act (HIPAA) might influence your choices if your client is in the health-care industry.

- **Competitiveness**—Many times your choices come down to ensuring that your business maintains an edge over the competition. New technology enables that to happen.

Before considering economic motivators for your device decisions, you should consider the technology forces. They often include the following:

- **Removal of borders**—Today, employees expect reliable data access from any location.

- **Virtualization**—Desktop, application, server, storage, and more are areas where virtualization is more pervasive than ever.

- **Growth of applications**—Customers expect new services and products, and improved customer support, all at a lower cost.

It is very helpful to break up the network into different areas as you are considering devices and their requirements. For example, you might choose the following for a large enterprise:

- Borderless

- Collaboration

- Data Center/Virtualization

Inside one of these groupings, further break down functional blocks. For example, you might divide the Borderless portion as follows:

- Policy and control

- Network services

- User services

- Connection management

Remember that your network is constantly evolving. In fact, Cisco Systems identifies a network life cycle that defines your work in phases over the span of the network's lifetime. Notice that this is a constantly revolving process, as shown in Figure 10-1.

Figure 10-1 *Cisco Network Lifecycle Model*

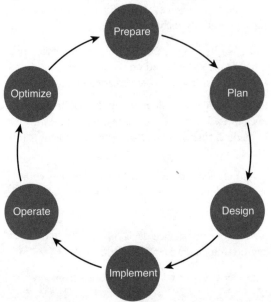

Environment Limitations—Network capabilities are dependent on their environment. Consider a small office/home office (SOHO) setting compared to that of a large corporate environment. Here are some key points to think about:

- Temperature controls and alerting might be lacking.
- Humidity controls and alerting might be deficient.
- There might not be adequate power—what about a UPS system?
- Wireless interference from neighboring locations is a possibility.

Equipment Limitations—If you are implementing a basic network as opposed to a more advanced one, you need to understand the restrictions of your equipment. Limitations might include these:

- Performance
- Redundancy
- Management
- Upgradeability

Compatibility Requirements—A huge challenge you face when implementing your network is ensuring that the devices and protocols you choose are compatible. Here are a few basic examples of just how complex this area can become:

- Your company needs to join with another organization and the network equipment must integrate. You are an all-Cisco shop running EIGRP as your routing protocol, but the company you are merging with is running OSPF.

- You have been instructed to implement a new network application. You have discovered that this application does not run on the server operating systems your company uses.

- You have been instructed to install a new hardware-based firewall in your network location. You have discovered that this firewall breaks several network applications in their default configurations.

Wired/Wireless Considerations—There are times when a wireless installation is ideal, and then there are times when it is definitely not. Here are just a few factors to consider when deciding between wired and wireless:

- **Security**—It is possible to achieve high levels of security with wireless networks, but it requires more planning and expertise than wired network infrastructures.

- **Performance**—It appears that wireless performance capabilities lag when compared to wired; analyzing the requirements of applications and your users is a critical step to ensure you are making the right choice.

- **Scalability**—Compare the ease of infrastructure growth of wired versus wireless to accommodate increased capacity.

- **Availability**—Determine whether the wireless network can feature the same levels of availability that are often seen with wired.

- **Cost**—Analyze the costs associated with installation and maintenance of wireless versus wired.

Security Considerations—Believe it or not, companies still overlook network security. Common misconceptions are that it is too difficult, expensive, or unnecessary.

At least be sure to carefully consider a security plan. The following tips can help you develop one:

- Focus on return on value rather than return on investment. Consider the harm a network security breach could do to your business, such as lost revenue or customer litigation.

- Never assume that network attacks will come only from outsiders. Your employees can accidentally create security vulnerabilities, and disgruntled or former employees can cause considerable damage.

- Don't be tempted to confront security concerns with a piecemeal approach rather than a single, unified strategy that protects your whole network.

- Work with others in your company to develop and roll out security strategies, focusing on technology, training, and physical site security with tools like surveillance cameras.

- Find the right balance between security and usability. The more secure your network is, the more difficult it can be to use.

You should have a written network security plan in place. A thorough policy should cover topics such as these:

- **Acceptable use policy**—Specify what types of network activities are allowed and which ones are prohibited.

- **E-mail and communications activities**—Help minimize problems from e-mails and attachments.

- **Antivirus policy**—Help protect the network against threats like viruses, worms, and Trojan horses.

- **Identity policy**—Help safeguard the network from unauthorized users.

- **Password policy**—Help employees select strong passwords and protect them.

- **Encryption policy**—Provide guidance on using encryption technology to protect network data.

- **Remote access policy**—Help employees safely access the network when working outside the office.

Chapter 11

Monitoring Tools

Networking continues to become more complex; therefore, you need a more robust set of monitoring tools. This chapter reviews some of the key tools and aspects of monitoring your network as proactively as possible.

Popular Monitoring Tools

Let's begin this chapter by examining the most popular tools.

Packet/Network Analyzer—Also termed a *protocol analyzer* or *network analyzer*, this tool is most often a combination of hardware and software that you install in a computer or network to improve protection against malicious activity. Network analyzers can supplement firewalls, antivirus programs, and spyware detection programs.

In addition to the tremendous security enhancements they offer, packet analyzers also help you learn about your network and network traffic, and how to pinpoint misconfigurations in the network.

Most packet analyzers can be utilized for the following tasks:

- Provide detailed statistics for current and recent activity on the network
- Test anti-malware programs and pinpoint potential vulnerabilities

- Detect unusual levels of network traffic and unusual packet characteristics

- Identify packet sources or destinations

- Configure alarms for defined threats

- Search for specific data strings in packets

- Monitor bandwidth utilization as a function of time

- Create application-specific plug-ins

- Display statistics in a user-friendly control panel

Interface Monitoring Tools—These tools monitor and report on the status or details regarding a network interface. Simple Network Management Protocol (SNMP) is an example of such a protocol. Problems such as garbled packets or unexpected line errors can be reported by an interface monitoring tool.

Port Scanner—This tool is used to identify opened listening ports on a network device. A recognized open port usually implies a network service that is running on that device. Port scanners used by an attacker might be looking for vulnerabilities. Port scanners used by the administrator can be used to locate unauthorized services that might be running on servers and/or workstations.

Top Talkers/Listeners—Tools like protocol and network analyzers can identify the top communicators on a network. This is usually sorted based on the type of traffic, such as Hypertext Transfer Protocol (HTTP) or File Transfer Protocol (FTP). A listener could be any device that has an open port listening or waiting for connection requests, and a talker could be a client making the request or a server providing services. The list of top talkers/listeners could be based on one of the following:

- Number of bytes sent

- Number of connections made

- Number of transactions completed

SNMP Management Software—This is a standards-based method used to gather information from network devices by using a command called **get**. SNMP-managed devices also generate alerts that can be sent to an SNMP manager. The host-initiated messages are called *traps*. A specific set of items that are managed by SNMP on a host are determined by the management information base (MIB). As a result, the SNMP manager might need to be configured to support multiple MIBs, based on the types of devices it is managing. When a query is sent from the SNMP manager distributed to all the objects in a MIB, it is referred to as *walking the SNMP MIB or using the walk feature to go through the entire MIB.*

Alerts—These are a method of becoming aware of a situation early enough to prevent disastrous results. Alerts can be generated by an SNMP system, as well as from many other management tools. Now, of course, alerts are not very beneficial if the administrator never knows about them. For that reason, many management tools include the capability to deliver alerts via e-mail messages, via SMS (text messages), or by calling a phone number when the severity of an alert is high enough to require that level of response. Alerts and alert actions can be configured by the administrator.

Packet Flow Monitoring—Many tools are used to collect and analyze the flow of traffic on the network. In addition to a protocol or network analyzer, you can use a method called NetFlow. This feature can be run on a switch or another networking device and reports to a collection service called a NetFlow collector, which is also on your network. The NetFlow collector produces graphs and charts to indicate the top talkers and top protocols in use on the network. Traffic patterns can be compared against the baseline and alerts set if current traffic patterns are abnormally different from that baseline, which might imply that there is a problem on the network or that the network is trending in a different direction than normal.

SYSLOG—System log messages, referred to as *syslog messages*, can be generated for events that occur on network devices, and sent to a centralized collection server referred to as a *syslog server*. Syslog messages include events such as when users log in to the system or when changes are made, or other events that occur on that system. Because syslog is an open standard, it can be used on network devices regardless of vendor, as long as the network device supports syslog messages.

SIEM (Security Information and Event Management)—This provides real-time analysis of alerts generated by security devices such as firewalls, and other network devices and systems that produce security logs. The consolidation and reporting of security events are also primary goals for security information and event management.

Environmental Monitoring Tools—Computing devices do not react well to extreme heat or cold temperatures. Proper heating, cooling, and humidity controls should be supervised using environmental monitoring tools. A well-defined tool should have the capability to generate alerts when thresholds are reached or exceeded (such as the temperature becoming too high) so that corrective action is taken to protect the computing environment. This applies to both data centers and wiring closets, where heat can be equally destructive.

Power Monitoring Tools—Clean power is often taken for granted. But when power is not clean or present, it is a recipe for disaster for a computing environment. Power monitoring tools should be able to identify abnormal fluctuations in power so that proper measures can be taken to protect the computing environment. Devices such as conditioners, generators, and battery backups can be deployed, and alerts should be generated when these devices have been activated.

Wireless Survey Tools—A typical deployment of a new wireless network uses a suite of wireless survey tools to identify competing access points, as well as the correct placement of new access points to allow adequate coverage for wireless users. These tools create what is known as a *heat map* to identify signals and their strengths in the wireless space. High-end wireless survey tools are dedicated devices, but it is also common to have wireless survey tools delivered as applications to smartphones.

Wireless Analyzers—This would very likely be one of the wireless survey tools that monitors the wireless space and strength of signals when creating a network design for wireless. A wireless analyzer can also be used for troubleshooting when an access point is no longer effective in covering an area. It can also detect rogue access points (unauthorized access points) that users or malicious individuals might have brought into the wireless space.

Metrics and Reports

Baseline—This is used as a reference point for comparison. A baseline specifies the average amount of various types of traffic that cross the network on an hourly basis. It can indicate the response time for an application being delivered from a server to get an answer to a client. A baseline could also represent a default set of rules that are applied to any new computer or device on the network. When a baseline has been established, changes made to the network or to the system can then be compared against the existing baseline to measure the impact of the new results to the existing baseline.

Bottleneck—This is also referred to as a *choke point* or a *holdup* in a network or system. An example is if you have Fast Ethernet everywhere in the network running at 100 Mbps but a server that is used by many people being connected at 10 Mbps and running at half-duplex. The access to the server causes a bottleneck, or a slowdown, due to this network configuration. If you have a bottleneck due to throughput on the wide area network, you should implement congestion management services such as traffic shaping and QoS. This prioritizes the traffic that absolutely must get there first, such as voice and other latency-sensitive traffic. Protocols that are not as critical would be affected more from the lack of bandwidth due to the bottleneck.

Log Management—Receiving events, alerts, and log messages from syslog, SNMP, or SIEM is very useful when you're correlating events from multiple devices. They collect and manage the data. Log management involves access control to determine who is allowed to see or delete log information. It also establishes rules to ensure its safekeeping.

Graphing—It is often said that a picture is worth a thousand words. Many tools, including NetFlow collectors, protocol analyzers, and other management tools, have the capability to create graphs and charts to represent the data for various purposes.

Utilization—Utilization means different things to different devices. For example, on a network you might measure bandwidth utilization in terms of how many bits per second are being sent compared to the capacity of that network segment. For storage such as iSCSI or Fibre Channel, you also have network concerns regarding utilization because the storage devices are accessed over a network. But you also have capacity on the storage devices themselves. On a computing device such as a server, you might want to monitor the utilization of the network device CPU, or the network device memory. On a wireless network you might want to monitor the utilization of the wireless channel that you are using to send and receive data on that Wi-Fi network.

Link Status—It is scientifically proven that an interface connected to a link such as a wide area network link can send more data if the link is up and active instead of down. Link status refers to the health of the link that an interface, such as a router interface, is connected to. Monitoring tools such as SNMP are used to track link status and generate an alert if the link status is down.

Interface Monitoring—This can be very detailed and proceed beyond just the status of the interface. The following details can be monitored and reported based on the type of interface being examined:

- Errors
- Utilization
- Discards
- Packet drops
- Interface resets
- Link speed
- Duplex

If an interface should be operating at full duplex and 100 Mbps, but is operating at half-duplex and 10 Mbps, that causes a significant bottleneck for the device with this interface when the network starts to get busy. By receiving alerts, an administrator could investigate and correct the problem regarding the speed and duplex.

Configuration Management Resources

Archives/Backups—There are only two types of computer users: users who have lost data and users who will lose data. Having an archive (a backup) of critical systems, including servers, routers, firewalls, switches, and other network devices, is key in delivering information to users. It is critical for every company to have an automated system that can back up and verify that process. Periodic spot checks should be performed to confirm that a restore can be done using the archives and backups that were previously created. These can be tested on virtualized machines. The management of backups is also important because of the data that they hold. Some backup systems have encryption to protect confidentiality, whereas others rely on secure storage to protect the content. Off-site methods using either physical or digital storage in another location can be used to protect the backed-up data in the event of physical destruction to the local facility.

Baselines—This refers to a set of rules and settings for a new system or device that is being placed on the network. A baseline configuration can help avoid unnecessary and insecure protocols that might otherwise be enabled or allowed on that system. It can also assist with the hardening of a device before it is customized and put into production. An automated method for deploying a baseline can be accomplished through a virtualized setup of computers. One example is a virtualized desktop infrastructure (VDI) in which the virtual machines reside in the data center, but the users are at their desks or remotely connected from another location.

On-boarding and Off-boarding of Mobile Devices—Bring your own device (BYOD) can create a lot of problems for a corporate network. Procedures that integrate personal devices on a corporate network (on-boarding) help ensure that data protection for company resources and company data is in place.

One example is to install agents or specialized software on the mobile devices that provide additional security or are required for integration with the company network. Mobile devices might be owned by the user or they might be owned by the company and assigned to the user. In either case, an on-boarding policy should be in place. Because technology changes and users don't always stay with the same company, an off-boarding policy should also be ready to remove any company data from mobile devices, and restrict or prevent access to a mobile device that was previously on the network but is no longer. This can include access control lists or other technical controls that can either allow or deny specific devices network access.

NAC—Network Admission Control provides access to the network and restricts entry based on a set of requirements. Here are two examples:

■ A requirement that every computer must contain an up-to-date virus protection program. If this is not implemented, access to the network is not allowed.

■ A requirement that the registry of a Windows computer must include specific characters that have been placed there previously by the network team. If these characters are not present, the network denies access to that device.

Network Admission Control can be implemented at the port level on a switch, as well as other common access methods that networked devices initially use to gain access to the network.

Documentation—Having clear and up-to-date documentation is critical for maintaining security and troubleshooting for a network. Details such as network diagrams (logical/physical) should be created and maintained and easily accessible. Inventory management, sometimes referred to as *asset management*, should be documented and can include the following:

■ Serial numbers of devices

■ Details regarding designated persons assigned to the asset

■ The IP addressing scheme, including the quantity of IP addresses available and IP address utilization

These documented elements will ensure that you correctly plan for network growth when devices might exceed the current capacity of an IP network segment.

For warranty work or third-party service contracts or agreements, make sure that you have proper vendor documentation regarding any equipment or service agreements that are currently in place. This should include contract numbers that might be needed when support cases are opened with a vendor. Records regarding acceptable use policies (AUP) should be clearly documented and signed by each user on the network. Internal operating procedures/policies/standards should also be clearly reported, communicated, and agreed to. This includes incident-handling procedures that identify the exact steps to be followed when a potential incident, problem, or security concern occurs.

Chapter 12

Network Segmentation

There are many advantages to implementing network segmentation, including security, testing, and maintaining compliance. This chapter explores several scenarios that would benefit from network segmentation.

SCADA Systems/Industrial Control Systems—A Supervisory Control and Data Acquisition (SCADA) system is an example of an industrial control system. This is computer-based and monitors and controls industrial structures such as manufacturing plants, power generation, and water treatment facilities. It is critical that communications over the network used for control and monitoring not be interrupted or compromised.

One method of helping to maintain the integrity of the system is to isolate it from other networks, such as data networks supporting end users. When you keep the SCADA system or industrial control system network separate, there is less opportunity for interference or malicious (or nonmalicious) access. Also, within a SCADA system, it is very likely that the communications between the control center and the equipment being monitored and controlled will be isolated or segmented from the management and communications with other devices or equipment in that same network. This isolation also helps to prevent a total collapse if there is a single fault in the network.

Legacy Systems—This is a system that has been in place for an extended period. It might be using outdated hardware or software but can still be a critical resource in the network. Because it is a legacy system, it might not have the protection that current hardware and software can provide. It also might be using legacy protocols that are less secure, such as Telnet or FTP, which are plaintext insecure protocols. When possible, it is desirable to disable insecure protocols. At the very least, you should separate these legacy systems from more current production networks. The isolation between legacy systems and the current network provides additional protection because an attacker would first have to gain access to the network on which the legacy system resides.

Separate Private/Public Networks—Many corporations have Wi-Fi as well as wired connectivity as part of their network resources. Ideally, these networks could be implemented as different subnets in different VLANs. The routers connecting these VLANs and subnets could use access control lists to filter and control the traffic that is allowed to cross between those networks. In addition, if guest access is going to be allowed, a separate VLAN and subnet that would very likely be Wi-Fi should be set up for the guest users. Keeping the guest network separate from the private network is an example of isolation. This improves the security of the private network. A company would also want to set up firewall services to monitor, protect, and filter traffic that is allowed between the private network, the Internet, and any other public networks.

Honeypot/Honeynet—It is extremely likely that attackers will use port scanners to attempt to illegally connect to resources that are accessible over public networks such as the Internet. So a company can set up a honeypot. It is a server with open ports and services that look, to the outside world, as a typical server. However, the honeypot does not have any sensitive data that could be used to compromise the company.

The benefits of having a honeypot include logging data and gaining possible insight to future attacks. Records can be kept regarding ports that are being scanned, attempted or completed logins, and other compromising actions that an attacker might take against a real server that might contain or have access to sensitive data. A honeynet is a collection of honeypot servers that are located at one site or multiple sites. The separation and isolation aspect of a honeypot is to keep attackers busy with noncritical servers, which should prevent or at least delay them from getting to the production servers.

Testing Lab—Anytime a change needs to be made to a production network, it should be analyzed in a testing lab first. This is also true when performing development on software or testing systems regarding security. Testing changes and then comparing the results against existing baselines will prepare you for more accurate results when those changes are actually deployed in the production network. The testing lab should be isolated from the production network so that any modifications made in the lab don't impact the production network.

Load Balancing—If there are multiple servers that contain the same content, it makes sense to distribute the requests for that content across the multiple servers. This is accomplished by using a load balancer that is placed between the servers and the clients making the requests. Typical examples of popular load balancers currently include F5 and Citrix's NetScaler products. The process of load balancing is generally transparent to the end user. You can isolate the servers on the back end from the users who are making the request. This separation enables you to send resource requests to multiple servers in a round-robin fashion. Or you can forward a request to a specific server based on the type of client that is making the request by analyzing the request as it comes in.

Performance Optimization—Network engineers strive for redundancy and reliability while trying to achieve the optimum results from a system or network, so it is important to correctly size the networks. For example, if a single subnet and VLAN have 400 users and there is a problem with that VLAN, there is potential impact to all 400 users. By creating smaller subnets in each VLAN, you create smaller fault domains, and as a result, if there is a problem it would impact a lesser number of users. Also, the size of the networks can affect performance if the servers are all in the same network as the users. By isolating users to a set of VLANs and subnets while placing the servers in separate VLANs and subnets, you can control access on the router interfaces between those networks. This can prevent a full system failure when one of the user subnets is having a problem.

Security—Unauthorized entry is possible only if there is access. On networks you can create separate subnets and VLANs for users who have similar needs on the network. Use access control lists on router interfaces to control and filter the traffic that is allowed between the subnets. This type of isolation improves security. You can also prevent users' access to the network until they authenticate at a switch port. This type of isolation stops users from participating on the network until they have authenticated successfully.

Compliance—In many systems, including those that are subject to regulation from government or other organizations, companies might need to implement isolation between various parts of the network to maintain compliance. This leads to better security for the system.

Chapter 13

Patches and Updates

Updates to systems and applications are common occurrences in today's networks. When you are making any changes to a system, server, or network, it is important to verify that the modification being implemented won't impact security, performance, or functionality in any negative way. Whenever possible, you should test the upgrade, update, or patch in a test environment before rolling it out to production. You should always have and follow documented change control procedures.

OS (Operating System) Updates—These can be either major or minor updates, depending on what is being changed in the OS. In a test environment, verify whether the applications and services that were used on the older operating system still function correctly. If they do not, or if there are security concerns regarding the revised operating system, those issues should be resolved before the new operating system updates are rolled out.

Firmware Updates—This might be necessary to correct a security flaw or performance issue, or simply to correct an existing bug. Full testing in a lab environment should be performed before the update on the production network devices. It is also recommended that once tested, the firmware update is implemented in only a small portion of the network. That way, if any issues arise in the production network regarding the update, it can be identified before the complete update across all devices in the network. There should also be a rollback procedure, one that has been documented and tested, that would allow an administrator to revert to a previous version of the firmware if needed.

Driver Updates—These update individual components on a system such as video, network, or disk drive systems. They should also be thoroughly tested before being implemented on a production network. If a driver update causes an application to fail, and if the driver update is not critical, you should roll back to the previous driver version. A driver update should not require that other applications and services also be updated.

Feature Changes/Updates—This is an update that applies new features to a server or system. Full testing should be completed to verify whether security concerns have been met, and that the feature change/update does not negatively impact current functionality.

Major Versus Minor Updates—A major update might be, say, going from version 2.2 to version 3.0, and might require a complete reinstallation of the software. This would deserve significant analysis and verification in a test environment regarding security and functionality. When a major update is performed, user training regarding differences in the system should also be implemented. A minor update might be going from version 2.2 to version 2.3. It still should be tested in a lab environment, though it is less likely to introduce problems.

Vulnerability Patches—This has a high priority for implementation. An attacker might have an advantage against an unpatched system. Even though there is an urgent need for the application of a vulnerability patch, testing in a lab environment is absolutely critical so that larger problems are not introduced to the network.

Upgrading Versus Downgrading—One of the first rules in making a configuration change, or implementing an update or a patch, is to have a configuration backup. You should also have a software backup of the software or system that is being upgraded. Testing should also be done to verify the procedure for downgrading, which is the process of restoring the previous version. Specify a time frame for upgrading, as well as the necessary time for downgrading, if it needs to be done. As a general rule, an upgrade or a patch should be able to stand on its own, without the need for changing other drivers or applications that worked before that upgrade or patch. If an upgrade or a patch causes problems, you should downgrade the system, or have the patch removed, instead of trying to upgrade a set of additional drivers and software to become compatible with the upgrade that was just performed. The release notes for updates and upgrades should list prerequisites regarding software and hardware that must be in place to make the update or upgrade successful.

Chapter 14

Implementing Switches

Managed switches, which make Layer 2 switching possible in high-speed Ethernet networks, are critical in a corporate infrastructure. This chapter examines several features that are used with Layer 2 switches.

VLAN (Virtual Local Area Network)—This can be used to separate a group of computing devices from each other, even if those devices are on the same physical switch. A VLAN provides isolation among networking devices. Another name for a VLAN is a *Layer 2 broadcast domain*. Typically, each VLAN is associated with a separate and unique IP subnetwork address. VLANs are controlled and implemented on the Layer 2 switches. Individual switch ports are assigned as access ports associated with a specific VLAN. The default VLAN assignment for access ports on a switch is VLAN 1.

Spanning Tree (802.1D)/Rapid Spanning Tree (802.1w)—Spanning Tree Protocol (STP) is used to identify parallel paths in a Layer 2 network, which has the potential to create a Layer 2 loop if not prevented. Spanning Tree blocks on one or more ports as needed to prevent traffic from forwarding on parallel paths in the switched network. 802.1D was the original Spanning Tree Protocol that was created decades ago. Since then, many new and improved standards have been implemented, including Rapid Spanning Tree, which is known as *802.1w*. When a switch receives a frame and the switch does not know the specific port that should be used, the switch uses a process called *flooding* to forward the frame to all other ports associated with that same VLAN. When a switch receives a frame, and knows which port to use to reach the destination MAC address in the Layer 2 frame, the switch forwards the frame only on that port, and filters (prevents) the frame from being sent on other ports in that same VLAN.

Interface Configuration—A switch interface can be configured with fixed speed and duplex, or it can be allowed to automatically negotiate the speed and duplex to use between the switch port and the device connected to the switch port. Full duplex enables simultaneous sending and receiving between the device and the switch port. Using the highest common speed supported by both the switch port and the device connected to it also provides optimal throughput when used with full duplex.

An interface on a switch can be configured as an access port and assigned to a single VLAN. This is referred to as the *VLAN assignment* of a port.

If there are interfaces that are being used to connect two switches, they can be configured as trunk ports and use a feature called *trunking* between the two switches. Trunk ports enable the traffic from multiple VLANs to cross between the two switches, without requiring a separate physical link for each VLAN being supported. To identify the correct VLAN, when a frame is being sent over the trunk, the sending switch includes an 802.1Q tag, similar to a header, for each frame that is being sent. Included inside this 802.1Q tag is the VLAN number associated with the frame being sent. This is called a *tagged* frame. The two switches that are configured with trunk ports connecting to each other can also identify a special VLAN referred to as the *native* VLAN. When traffic associated with the native VLAN is sent over the trunk, the switches do not include an 802.1Q tag for frames associated with the native VLAN. This is referred to as an *untagged* VLAN. Untagged frames are presumed to belong to the native VLAN. When using 802.1Q trunking in a Cisco environment, an additional protocol called *VLAN Trunk Protocol* (VTP) could also be used. VTP enables the synchronization and automatic creation or deletion of VLANs on multiple switches as long as there are functioning trunks between the switches, when the VTP protocol is enabled.

If there are two links between a pair of switches, Spanning Tree identifies the parallel paths and as a result blocks one of them. This reduces throughput. An alternative is to use a technique referred to as *port bonding*, using Link Aggregation Control Protocol (LACP), to logically group the ports into one logical interface. With a single logical interface between the two switches, Spanning Tree will no longer block. Therefore, it allows more bandwidth between the two switches because both links are available to forward traffic between the two switches.

It is often recommended to remotely connect to a switch, using an IP address, to manage a switch. The switch needs an IP address for this to occur. To assign an IP address, the switch uses a logical interface associated with one of its VLANs. This interface is referred to as a *VLAN interface*, or a *switched virtual interface* (SVI). An IP address is assigned to the VLAN interface to allow an administrator to remotely connect to the switch.

The switch can also allow an administrator to perform protocol analysis by replicating the data that is seen on a VLAN. The switch can collect and send the collected data to a port where a computer, running a protocol analyzer, collects and examines the data. The replication performed by the switch is referred to as *port mirroring* (but can also apply to entire VLANs). Local mirroring occurs when the switch collects data from local ports or local VLANs and sends the collected data to another port on the same physical switch. Remote mirroring happens when the collected data is gathered on a remote switch and forwarded to a physically different switch, where the protocol analyzer is connected to one of that switch's ports.

Default Gateway—If a switch is managed remotely and has an IP address configured on it, it also needs a default gateway to be able to reply to administrators' requests, when those requests are coming from a different subnet than the switch's management IP address. The default gateway for a switch serves the same purpose as a default gateway used by a computer. It simply allows reachability to networks beyond the local network to which the switch is connected.

PoE (Power over Ethernet) and PoE+ (802.3af, 802.3at)—This is a fantastic way to use the switch port to deliver power over the networking cables to devices such as cameras and IP telephones. The earlier standard of 802.3af delivered up to 15.4 watts of DC power, and the newer 802.3at standard provides up to 25.5 watts of power.

Switch Management—If switches are managed remotely, they need an IP address assigned to a VLAN interface as well as a default gateway. When administrators remotely connect to the switch logically, they are connecting a virtual terminal (VTY) on that switch. By increasing the number of virtual terminals, you can expand the number of administrators that could simultaneously be remotely connected to, and logged in to, the switch. To protect the switch, safeguards such as required usernames and passwords should be set in place before access is allowed.

One method to set up users and passwords is to create user accounts on each switch. In larger environments this becomes tedious and hard to maintain. A more scalable solution is to design a centralized user database for administrators on a server built for authentication authorization and accounting (AAA). Then the switch can check with the AAA server to verify usernames and passwords before allowing administrative access to the switch. When connecting to the switch for administration of the switch, over the same network as the users, it is referred to as *in-band management*. If a separate and isolated network was set up for the sole purpose of managing network devices, including the switch, it is an example of *out-of-band management*. This is an example of isolation that improves security. On most devices, including managed switches, there is usually a console port. If an administrator is physically next to the switch, they could connect to the console port using a cable from their PC to the switch console port for management of that switch. Username and password protection should be implemented on this console port, as well as the virtual terminal lines that are used to administratively access the switch remotely.

Managed Versus Unmanaged—A managed switch can be connected by the administrator locally using the console port, or remotely via a virtual terminal using an IP address. A managed device has a configuration that can be manipulated or changed by an administrator. An unmanaged switch does not allow local or remote administration, and has no configurable parameters. It is basically taken out of the box, plugged in to a power source, and then used as a basic Layer 2 switch to allow connectivity among the devices that are connected to it. An unmanaged switch is significantly less expensive than a managed switch. Most corporate environments use managed switches that can be configured with features such as Port Security, multiple VLANs, and trunking.

Chapter 15

Implement a Wireless LAN

Wireless technology is becoming more prevalent and uses radio frequency to transmit data to and from network devices. This chapter examines several concepts as they relate to wireless local area networks (WLAN).

Small Office/Home Office Wireless Router—This integrates ports for Layer 2 switching and Layer 3 routing (between the Internet and the local area network), as well as wireless capabilities to receive and send to wireless network devices inside the home or small office. Generally, the wireless devices and those connected to the switch port are in the same logical IP network and the same VLAN.

Wireless Access Points—An access point, also known as an *AP*, has an Ethernet network interface adapter that enables the access point to be connected physically to a switch port. The wireless access point also includes one or more antennas that permit it to send and receive radio frequency to support wireless clients. When planning a wireless network, you should determine the approximate number of clients that will be using a single access point (device density) and the amount of traffic to be sent and received by those clients. If there is too much of a demand on an access point, it might affect network performance.

In a larger environment a company might have multiple access points working with each other to provide seamless access. This benefits a wireless client who might be moving a wireless device, such as a laptop or a smartphone, between the ranges of the individual access points. Moving between access points is referred to as *roaming*. The coordinated effort to allow roaming and other enhanced features that involve multiple access points uses a device called a *wireless controller* or *a wireless LAN controller* (WLC). A user connects to the network through an access point and is assigned to a virtual local area network (VLAN). To keep the size of VLANs relatively small, multiple VLANs can be used, and as users authenticate to the wireless network they can be assigned or associated with one of the many VLANs available. The capability to round-robin and place users in one of many VLANs is referred to as *VLAN pooling*. In an organization where wireless LAN controllers are used, special protocols are implemented to communicate between the access points and the wireless LAN controller. One protocol is the Lightweight Access Point Protocol (LWAPP). In a Cisco environment the protocol used between an access point and the wireless LAN controller is called CAPWAP, which stands for Control and Provisioning of Wireless Access Points.

Wireless Bridge—If a wireless client is located too far away from the access point, a wireless bridge can be used. It acts like a repeater as it receives and regenerates signals between the access point and the wireless client.

Site Surveys—This is often performed before a wireless network is implemented but can also be done afterward. A site survey measures the strength of the signals being generated by the access points to confirm that there is adequate coverage for wireless networking in the desired areas. It also documents which frequencies the access points are currently using. The results are often used to create what is known as a *heat map* that shows a visual representation of the present signals and their strength. The heat map does not reflect the temperature but rather the radio frequencies that are present in the area.

Frequencies—Several frequencies are available for WLANs. The two major groups of frequencies are in the 2.4 GHz and 5 GHz ranges. These are freely used by entities including companies for their wireless networking. Because multiple companies that might be very close in proximity to each other can use these frequencies, site surveys and planning must be done to optimize the efficiency and decrease the interference by other access points that are not part of the company.

Channels—In the 2.4 GHz range the number of channels or sections of frequencies that are available depends on the country and equipment capabilities. In the United States channels 1, 6, and 11 are considered to be nonoverlapping channels. If three access points are right next to each other and one is using channel 1, another channel 6, and the third channel 11, they will not interrupt each other or overlap from a frequency perspective.

Goodput—This refers to the application layer throughput after the overhead of an underlying protocol is taken away. For example, if a network has the capacity to move data at 54 Mbps, but the overhead took 14 Mbps, then goodput is around 40 Mbps.

Connection Types—Many different technologies are used for WLANs. These include the 802.11 family of b, a, g, n, and ac. In 802.11a-ht and 802.11g-ht, the "ht" stands for "high throughput."

Make sure that when you deploy a WLAN both the access points and the clients can support the specific technology that you plan on implementing.

Even though an access point is capable of implementing HT, the wireless clients must also have the capacity for high-throughput features.

Antenna Placement—The antenna placement for the access points should be determined by an appropriate wireless site survey. The antenna's location should provide appropriate coverage for the company's clients. Some antennas are internal to the access point, whereas others are physically visible. There might be a single antenna or multiple antennas.

Antenna Types—These include omnidirectional, unidirectional, and directional antennas. An omnidirectional antenna sends and receives radio frequency in all directions surrounding the access point.

Unidirectional is desirable when the radio frequencies need to be directed in a specific area. The following are examples:

- An antenna between two buildings
- An antenna inside one building that faces away from a parking lot to provide wireless access inside the building but not in the parking area

A Yagi antenna is an example of a unidirectional wireless antenna.

MIMO/MUMIMO—802.11n and 802.llac both use multiple antennas to send and receive multiple streams simultaneously. This technique is referred to as *multiple in multiple out* (MIMO). 802.11n supports four streams simultaneously, while 802.11ac provides eight streams concurrently. 802.11ac also supports a feature called *multi-user MIMO* (MU-MIMO). When 802.11ac is used with an 80 MHz channel, each channel can support close to 400 Mbps. To achieve gigabit performance, only three of the channels (out of a possible eight) need to be used.

Signal Strength—Similar to listening to a radio station in your car, in which case the farther away you drive, the weaker the signal is, wireless radio frequency signals also degrade when distanced from the source, including the access point. If a signal or signals need to propagate through walls or other objects, that also minimizes the signal. For a small area, a centralized access point with an omnidirectional antenna might be sufficient if there are no obstructions between the access point and the wireless clients who are using it. If connectivity between buildings is required, a likely candidate is a unidirectional antenna. It focuses the sending and receiving in one direction. That direction would be toward the other building, which also would have an antenna mounted either to the outside or on top. The distance to be covered by an access point is determined by the amount of power being used, obstacles in the path, other interfering signals, and frequencies being used. Generally, higher frequencies do not travel as far as lower frequencies.

SSID Broadcast—A wireless network can be identified by a wireless client through its service set identifier (SSID). In an enterprise environment there can be multiple access points that are all supporting a single SSID. It's also possible that with a single access point you could create multiple SSIDs; for example, one for corporate users and another isolated and separate wireless network with a separate SSID for guests.

Topologies—In most corporations that are using wireless, access points are used in what is known as *infrastructure mode*. The access point enables the extension of the existing infrastructure for wireless clients. For example, if a wireless client was connected to an access point working in infrastructure mode, that client would then have access based on the permissions to other network resources on the wired network. This includes servers and printers and other common network devices. It is also possible that two computers without any access point could build a small ad hoc network to communicate with each other. This isn't as secure, because the ad hoc network has been set up and managed by the users of those computers, and it is very likely that security wasn't a high priority for those users. Another type of wireless network is referred to as a *mesh network*. This is similar to an ad hoc network, in that there is not a centralized infrastructure being extended by the access point. Instead the mesh network is extended further by adding more devices (typically laptops) that have wireless capabilities to extend the network. The coverage area of the devices in the network can be thought of as a mesh cloud. If a single device removes itself from the network because of congestion, other devices in the network should be unaffected.

Mobile Devices—The demand for wireless has skyrocketed, primarily due to the fact that so many end-user devices, consumer products, and corporate computing devices have wireless capabilities integrated in them. This includes smartphones, laptops, PDAs, tablets, gaming devices, and media tools from various vendors, all with the capability to connect to wireless networks.

Chapter 16

Network Security Overview

Because the data that information systems carry is often confidential, it is important to maintain network security.

Disaster Recovery—The concept of disaster recovery is to minimize the impact of a disaster or disruption to the business. A recovery plan is used to quickly restore the company's systems.

Business Continuity—A business continuity plan enables a business to restore and/or remain functional in spite of a disruption. A business continuity plan usually includes a disaster recovery plan, as well as details for other significant events such as a cyber attack or major security breach, which if not handled correctly could force the company to close.

Battery Backups/UPS—Electricity and power are key components in data centers, networks, and computer systems. In anticipation of power failure, uninterruptible power supplies (UPS) should be implemented to supply power to critical systems short term. Additional generators should be planned for and implemented to provide longer-term power beyond what the battery-powered UPS can deliver.

First Responders—Disaster recovery plans should include incident handling procedures that indicate the selected first responders when a disruptive event occurs. First responders should know their responsibilities and the correct procedures to follow. This helps to minimize mistakes and risks when incidents occur.

Data Breach—This occurs when confidential information is made available to unauthorized parties. A data breach could be accidental or a result of a specific attack to obtain data. Attacks can be launched by internal users (disgruntled employees) or outsiders using social engineering and technical tools.

End-User Awareness and Training—End users are often the weakest link in many security systems. As a result, technical controls should be in place to limit access to them. User awareness training should be implemented, and verified, for anyone who has access to the company systems, such as e-mail file systems and databases. Part of a training and awareness program should include the ability to identify or recognize when a security incident has occurred, or when a suspicious e-mail has been received by a user.

Single Point of Failure—This implies that one component of a network or system, if it fails, causes a complete failure for the rest of the system. The major reason that single points of failure are not removed is cost. Fault tolerance and high availability can be implemented using techniques such as redundant power supplies and redundant routers, servers, and networks that connect those systems. Cost is often justified for fault tolerance and high availability because you are protecting critical assets and nodes in the networks.

Adherence to Standards and Policies—Some organizations are regulated by governing bodies. In this case, periodic auditing should be performed by a third party to verify whether the systems and networks are in compliance with the current standards, policies, and regulations. Companies often will implement their own standards and policies, and have users sign an acceptable use agreement regarding access to the system and networks.

Vulnerability Scanning—This is a proactive measure performed by network administrators. A typical vulnerability scanning system looks for services and/or ports that are available or open on systems that are not permitted. It can also scan a system for malicious or unauthorized software that might be present, either on the disk or in memory, with the intent of identifying and stopping the unauthorized activity or service.

Penetration Testing—This is used to verify the effectiveness of a company's current security policy and technology. For example, a company that implements a network-based intrusion prevention system might want to verify whether it is correctly identifying and preventing certain types of an attack. For verification, the company can hire a third-party penetration testing company, with instructions to use certain attacks against specific systems. On a much larger scale, the company performing the testing might have few or no restraints regarding what they can attempt to do. The benefit of this process is that if there are vulnerabilities, they can be identified and corrected before an actual attack from an unauthorized party.

Denial of Service (DoS) Attacks—This is an attempt to disable a service that otherwise should be available. For example, a DoS attack against a web server is not for the purpose of stealing data from the server, but rather to make it unavailable so that no one can access it.

When a DoS attack is being launched as a unified effort and is using hundreds, or thousands, of individual systems to launch the attack, it is referred to as a *Distributed DoS* (DDoS). This coordinated attack can use many different methods, including consumption of all the bandwidth that a server or system typically has available, by the hundreds or thousands of attacking systems sending and requesting data as part of the attack. When a traffic spike is generated, the real users of that system are unable to access that server or system and its resources.

A group of computers that have been compromised, and then used as part of a DDoS attack, is known as a *botnet*. These attacks typically leverage popular existing protocols and services. For example, when a ping request is sent, the receiver generally replies, if enabled for replying to ping requests, to the IP address of the device that sourced that packet. If an attacker's ping request was crafted so that the actual source address being used in the ping request is not the attacker's source IP address but that of some other device out on the Internet (a spoofed source address), the reply to the ping could be directed to the other device that wasn't expecting a ping reply. This type of an attack with a single ping is not devastating.

However, if the ping was directed to an entire network or subnetwork address that had hundreds or thousands of devices in it, and they all replied to that one host on the Internet, this type of amplified attack could cause a denial of service on the device that never sent the ping request in the first place. This attack is referred to as a *Smurf attack*. It is both a reflection- and an application-based attack. The reflection refers to the attacker delivering the attack by reflecting it off of a third-party network that's responding to the ping requests. It's an amplification attack due to the sheer quantity of devices that will deliver that ping response to the unsuspecting victim.

An amplification-and-reflection attack could also leverage the domain name system (DNS). The attacker could have a botnet that sends DNS requests out to the Internet and falsifies (spoofs) the source IP address. If there are 30,000 DNS requests going out to the Internet from the botnet, all the responses to those DNS queries are delivered to the victim.

This same type of technique of amplification and reflection could also be used with network time protocol (NTP). This occurs by spoofing the source IP address, which in turn has hundreds or thousands of NTP replies going back to a single address that never requested that information.

Sometimes a DoS attack is implemented unintentionally by a user. It might happen when users experiment with software and don't realize the impact. This can be prevented through proper user training, awareness, and acceptable user policies. A permanent DoS attack impacts the system in such a damaging way that it is no longer usable even after a reboot.

The resolution for this type of an attack might require a complete reinstall of the system or replacement of hardware.

A permanent DoS stack could easily be implemented if there is physical access to the system and the server or system is manually destroyed.

ARP (Address Resolution Protocol) Cache Poisoning—Computers on Ethernet networks use ARP to dynamically learn the Layer 2 address of other devices in the same VLAN, in order to communicate.

If an attacker can convince other devices in the network that the attacker's Layer 2 address is the Layer 2 address of the server, the frames destined to the server are forwarded to the attacker. This enables the attacker to perform a man-in-the-middle attack and gain access to the traffic flow that was intended to be between the client and the server. The ARP cache is a place in memory where computers maintain and keep track of the Layer 2 addresses of other devices. By continually poisoning that Layer 2 information in the ARP cache, the attacker can continue to receive frames that otherwise would not be sent to the attacker's address.

Packet/Protocol Abuse—These are methods that take advantage of the way protocols operate. Examples include DoS attacks that could involve NTP and DNS. Other types of protocol and packet abuse include crafting packets that don't follow the standards in an attempt to cause an abnormal reaction by a server or system that is receiving those packets. This might result in the server releasing information that it otherwise wouldn't. It might also cause a DoS attack due to the system or server not correctly dealing with the misconstructed packets or protocols.

Spoofing—This is about falsifying information. In a Smurf attack, the attacker spoofs or lies about the source IP address so that the responses to the ping request are sent to the IP address that was spoofed in the original ping request from the attacker. ARP poisoning implements spoofing of Layer 2 Ethernet addresses.

Wireless—Because physical connections are not used between a wireless client and an access point, it's easy for attackers to present themselves as a valid wireless network. The intent is having a user connect to the attacker's wireless network and reveal usernames, passwords, and other information that can potentially compromise the entire system.

A *rogue AP* is an access point that is not authorized in the area in which it is currently operating. An example of a rogue AP is when an attacker or a user brings in his own access point and plugs in to the network and offers Wi-Fi services in the corporate environment.

An *evil twin* is when an attacker advertises a wireless network that is the same as, or similar to, the valid SSID (service set identifier) of the authorized network. Attackers lure users to connect to the rogue access point in an attempt to compromise the end user and/or her computer.

War driving is the process of documenting the wireless networks that are present, their signal strength, and the type of technology and security they are using. The reason it is called war driving and not a site survey is because the data is being collected from equipment that is in a vehicle that is slowly moving through a neighborhood, a business area, or other areas that have Wi-Fi signals present.

War chalking is the documentation that an individual leaves on walls or other areas to communicate to other individuals regarding networks (specifically wireless open networks) that are available in that area, which could lead to additional unauthorized access.

Bluejacking occurs when an unsolicited message is sent to a Bluetooth device, such as a mobile phone or laptop. On the flip side, if data is taken in an unauthorized fashion from a device leveraging Bluetooth, that technique is referred to as *bluesnarfing.*

The security of wireless networks has gotten better over the years, and currently the best standard to use for securing a wireless network is 802.11i, or WPA2 (Wi-Fi Protected Access 2) enterprise mode. Users' credentials are stored on a centralized server, commonly referred to as a *AAA* server. When an attempt to authenticate is made, a wireless LAN controller (WLC) communicates with the AAA server. The WLC often uses a protocol named RADIUS (Remote Authentication Dial-In User Service) to verify the user and to set up the keys for that client's ability to use encryption services on the wireless network. If a centralized RADIUS server is not available, WPA2 can still be used with a PSK (preshared key). Older flavors of encryption including Wired Equivalent Privacy (WEP) and WPA should not be used when WPA2 is available. These previous security techniques have known vulnerabilities and are subject to compromise. One method that is commonly used in home networks for easy security setup is Wi-Fi protected setup (WPS). However, there are known security vulnerabilities with WPS. As a result, in a corporate environment the feature of WPS should be disabled.

Brute Force—This occurs when an attacker using an automated process continues to try to guess username and password combinations, in an attempt to access a system. By attempting millions of combinations, including random characters as well as commonly used passwords from a dictionary, as part of a brute force attack, the attacker might compromise the system. To prevent this, limits should be placed on the number of login attempts allowed. Tough passwords should also be implemented to reduce the effectiveness of a brute force attack.

Session Hijacking—This occurs when an attacker steps in to take over an existing securely established session. For example, when a user connects to a banking website, authenticates, and is looking at his balance, the attacker using a combination of tools, including spoofing, intercepts that session and injects the commands to transfer funds.

Social Engineering—Because users are often the weakest link in security, social engineering is a technique that leverages the human factor. Attackers pose as a credible source to trick a user into divulging classified information. To protect against this, user awareness training should be provided, and periodically tested to verify its effectiveness.

Man-in-the-Middle—This is when the attacker intercepts the conversation between two devices for the benefit of seeing all the traffic that is going between them. There are many ways to accomplish this task, including ARP poisoning. Network devices can implement Layer 2 and Layer 3 spoofed protection to help reduce this risk. Authentication, before allowing communications, is also a method to minimize these attacks. Figure 16-1 shows a man-in-the-middle attack between two routers.

Figure 16-1 *A Man-in-the-Middle Attack*
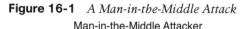
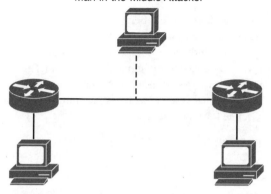

VLAN Hopping—This technique is used by an attacker to get direct access to a VLAN on a different IP subnet. Normally, multiple VLANs are created that are associated with various IP subnets. These VLANs and their IP subnets require IP routers to transmit packets between the different IP subnets and VLANs. By forcing this traffic through the router interfaces, you can apply access control lists (ACL) to those router interfaces to control the flow of traffic. When attackers circumvent the router interfaces, they can also bypass the access control lists on them. To protect against this risk, switch ports can be configured so that they do not have the capability to negotiate a trunk to an end-user device such as a PC.

Compromised System—This is a system that has released unauthorized information, or it could be a result of malicious software that has been run on a system, or from booting up to a nonstandard operating system through a removable drive such as a CD-ROM or thumb drive. In general, a system that is being compromised can no longer maintain data integrity, confidentiality, or availability regarding the data and services available through that system.

Effect of Malware on the Network—Malicious software, often referred to as *malware*, can compromise an entire system and commonly spreads to multiple systems. As malware propagates, additional traffic can be seen by an Intrusion Prevention System (IPS). An IPS can detect when requests for open ports are being made to network addresses that don't exist, including subnets that might not exist. Malware can collect keystroke information such as user login credentials (username and password), as well as other sensitive information. Some of the best solutions for malware include end-user awareness training and system-based software on each computer that detects malware. Network-based intrusion prevention systems can also identify signs of malware on the network.

Insider Threat/Malicious Employee—This is a huge risk for every company. For example, a person might take a position at a company for the sole purpose of gaining access to sensitive data. Disgruntled employees can become malicious. That's why every user should take part in awareness training to recognize signs of security incidents, including breaches of other employees, so that they can be correctly identified and reported. Users should also be given only enough access to systems and resources as are needed to perform their duties.

Zero Day Attacks—A zero day attack is tough to prevent because it is not well known by intrusion prevention systems or anti-malware software yet. Baselines can be created in systems, in computers, and on the network. Intrusion prevention software can examine traffic patterns that are abnormal, compared to a baseline, in an attempt to identify trends that might indicate that an attack is present. This same type of logic can also be applied to an individual system regarding programs run and memory utilization, compared to a baseline for that system.

Vulnerabilities—To reduce the risk of a vulnerability, countermeasures are implemented for protection. Examples of potential vulnerabilities and weaknesses may include the following:

- **Running unnecessary services**—You should avoid having unauthorized services such as FTP and web services, along with the open ports that correspond to those services, running on a system when they shouldn't be running.

- **Unpatched or an older legacy system**

- **Insecure protocols**—Moving data over the network without providing any encryption or protection is a risk. This could compromise usernames and passwords. These include the following:

  - Telnet
  - HTTP
  - SLIP
  - FTP
  - TFTP
  - SNMPv1
  - SNMPv2

  To mitigate or reduce the risk of using these clear-text protocols, secure counterparts such as SSH, HTTPS, SFTP, and SNMPv3 could be used.

- **Signals that are being generated by wireless network communications**—Wireless signals for a WLAN might be available to an attacker who is in a lobby or just outside a building. Use encryption services such as WPA2 for WLANs.

- **Emanation from wired networks**—An attacker with the correct resources could potentially collect the signals from networks, including the wired networks, without direct physical access to them. In environments that are so secure that you need to protect any emanation from leaking, a TEMPEST room (or rooms) could be used. TEMPEST is a national security agency and NATO certification. Its focus is to prevent leaking emanations including radio frequency (RF) and electrical signals, sounds, and vibrations from leaving the area where they are generated.

Chapter 17
Network Hardening

To reduce the effectiveness of attacks and misuse, security controls can be implemented and configurations made to improve the security posture for network devices and hosts that connect to those networks. This chapter covers many of those techniques.

Anti-Malware Software—This is intended to identify and prevent malicious software from running. Anti-malware software can be either host-based or network-based. Host-based software runs on a single computer and protects that computer. Network-based software runs on a device that is looking at all the traffic on the network to determine whether malware is being sent or received. A cloud-based anti-malware service can be used for dynamic updates.

Switch Port Security—Depending on the vendor, many security features might be implemented on a Layer 2 switch. These include the following:

- **DHCP snooping**—DHCP snooping protects the network against a rogue or malicious DHCP server from handing out IP address information and related options.

- **ARP inspection**—This prevents devices from misrepresenting or spoofing their Layer 2 MAC addresses, which might be done in an attempt to redirect traffic that is intended for one device on the network, to be sent to the attacker's address.

- **MAC address filtering**—This feature prevents certain MAC addresses from being permitted on the network. It could also allow only specific Layer 2 addresses to be permitted on the network.

- **VLAN assignments for network segmentation**—Individual switch ports that are configured as access ports for end-user devices can be assigned to specific VLANs. By organizing certain devices (servers) into one VLAN and other network devices (user computers) into a separate VLAN, additional security through isolation can be achieved. If traffic needs to go between two VLANs, a Layer 3 router can be used to route the packets, which by itself does not provide security. Adding access control lists to the router interfaces to specifically permit or deny certain traffic can be used to implement security between the VLANs and the IP subnets that are being used with those VLANs.

Security Policies—They should be created, and agreed to, by all users of the network for a clear understanding of what is allowed. User training is recommended to make users aware of possible security threats and how to report them.

Disable Unneeded Network Services—Web or file services that are running on a computer, but aren't needed or used, present a security risk. An attacker can search for these services and use them to gain additional access into the network. When a network service is not being used, it should be disabled.

Use Secure Protocols—Secure protocols should be used because they provide better security, including encryption and authentication. The following are some secure protocols:

- **SSH (Secure Shell)**—SSH provides remote terminal access, usually through a virtual terminal that is logically running on the router or switch being connected to for management. It requires authentication, and the session is encrypted so that even if eavesdroppers listen in on the conversation on the network, they won't have the keys to unlock and decode the data that's going back and forth.

- **SNMPv3 (Simple Network Management Protocol)**—This allows for the secure management and monitoring of network devices that support it. It provides authentication as well as encryption. Older SNMP protocols, such as version 1 and version 2, should be avoided because they are less secure.

- **TLS (Transport Layer Security)/SSL (Secure Socket Layer)**—They both represent a secure method of connecting to a web resource using the common HTTPS protocol.

- **SFTP (Secure File Transfer Protocol)**—SFTP is an extension of SSH that permits the transfer of files over a secured connection.

- **HTTPS**—Behind the scenes, HTTPS uses TLS or SSL for the security function.

- **IPsec**—This is a method used to protect a virtual private network (VPN).

The benefit of a VPN is that authentication and encryption can be implemented to provide confidentiality for data traveling over the virtual private network.

Access Lists—This list identifies what is, and is not, permitted through a given network interface. It applies to

- Web/content filtering
- Port filtering

- IPv4 filtering

- IPv6 filtering

When an access list is applied to an interface of a router, there is an implicit deny at the end of the access control list. In the list of permits and denies, if there is not a specific match in the access control list, the traffic or packet is denied because it doesn't match any of the entries in the access control list.

When an access control list is implemented, care must be taken to put the entries in the right order. When the traffic matches a line, the permit or deny (as contained in that access list entry) is executed and no further processing of the access control list is done for that packet. This means that if a specific deny statement is the very first line of an access control list, and later in that same access control there is a permit statement that would also match that same traffic, the packet is denied based on the match of the first line. Access control lists are processed beginning from the top.

Wireless Security—There are many standards and options for wireless security, which include the following:

- WEP—This is an older standard. It has weaknesses and vulnerabilities, and as a result should not be used.

- WPA/WPA2 (Enterprise and Personal)—WPA is an improved standard and has subsequently been updated with WPA2, which is also known as 802.11i. The enterprise version of WPA2 means that a centralized AAA server, such as a RADIUS server, is being employed for the authentication of the users. The personal version of WPA2 means that a preshared key is being used for the authentication instead of a centralized AAA server. In either case, WPA2 uses the Advanced Encryption Standard (AES) for encryption of the wireless traffic.

- TKIP (Temporal Key Integrity Protocol)/AES (Advanced Encryption Standard)—TKIP is a security protocol that was used help improve security. Now that more advanced standards such as WPA2 and AES are used, TKIP isn't as common. AES provides dramatic improvements in security with its powerful encryption capabilities. It also permits various levels of strength to be implemented.

- 802.1x—This is implemented to authenticate a user before giving the user further access in the network. This can be used with wireless networks as well as performing 802.1x at an access port on a Layer 2 switch.

- TLS (Transport Layer Security)/TTLS (Tunneled Transport Layer Security)— TLS and TTLS can be used to encrypt and protect traffic as it is sent over a network.

- MAC filtering—This permits the controlling of access to the network, based on the MAC address assigned to systems.

User Authentication—There are many ways to perform user authentication, including these:

- **CHAP (Challenge-Handshake Authentication Protocol)/MS-CHAP (Microsoft's implementation of CHAP)**—One of the benefits of CHAP with PPP is that during authentication CHAP does not send the user's password in clear text over the network, making it more secure.

- **PAP (Password Authentication Protocol)**—PAP is considered a weaker and less secure method to use with a PPP network. PAP does send the password in clear text during the authentication process. PAP and CHAP are typically used when connecting over a network that uses Point-to-Point Protocol (PPP) as the Layer 2 protocol.

- **EAP (Extensible Authentication Protocol)**—It is used for many authentication applications, including 802.1x.

- **Kerberos**—This is a popular authentication mechanism that is used on Microsoft Active Directory networks.

- **Multifactor authentication**—This requires more than a single item for user verification. Multifactor authentication has three categories, or factors:

  - Something the person knows, such as a password

  - Something the user has, such as an access card

  - Something the user is, such as having a unique fingerprint

  This type of authentication requires two or more of these to be presented by a user for authentication. An example would be presenting an access card and also having to punch in a code to enter a room. The card is something the user has, and the code is something the user knows.

- **Two-factor authentication**—This is an example of multifactor authentication that requires two of the three factors.

- **Single sign-on**—This method only requires a user to authenticate a single time to access the system. It allows all the access that the user is entitled to, without having to reauthenticate multiple times to access additional resources that are part of the network. Kerberos is an example of an authentication mechanism that provides the capability to have single sign-on (SSO).

Hashes—Popular hash examples include MD5 (Message Digest 5) and SHA (Secure Hash Algorithm). Hashing algorithms verify data integrity. For example, if you downloaded a file from Cisco Systems and plan to apply it as an update to a router or switch, how do you know that the file wasn't from a fake site or hasn't been corrupted? If a hash on the file is generated, it can be compared to the vendor's posted hash. If the hashes match, the file has data integrity and has not been modified from the original file being offered by the vendor.

Physical Security Controls—These controls include the following:

- **Mantrap**—This is an area the user must go through to enter a room or building. Typically there is a single entrance and exit, and there's room for only one person. The purpose of this is to force individual authentication, and if that authentication fails, the user is effectively trapped, which might require a security officer to intervene.

- **Network closet**—Also referred to as an *intermediate distribution frame* (IDF) or a *wiring closet*, is likely to be on every floor of a building. This is where the patch panels, cabling, and switches that support that floor are kept. Physical security controls should be implemented on the door to the wiring closet to prevent unauthorized access.

- **Video monitoring**—This can be a deterrent against unauthorized access, especially if there are clearly marked signs to indicate that video monitoring is in progress.

- **IP cameras/CCTVs (closed-circuit televisions)**—Typically, video monitoring is performed with either IP-based cameras or CCTVs. In many environments a security guard is hired to supervise a group of monitors that are receiving the images from the cameras and CCTV systems.

- **Door access controls**—These include physical locks, as well as proximity readers that can sense an access card. Entry to sensitive parts of the building, including the data center, should be logged and reviewed periodically.

- **Proximity reader/key fob**—A key fob or an access card could be issued to employees to allow them access into rooms or a building. They are used with a proximity reader for admittance. The proximity reader doesn't require physical contact with the key fob or access card; it only must be close to the reader.

- **Biometrics**—This is one of the factors in multifactor authentication. Biometrics refer to an identifiable body part of the user, such as a fingerprint, a retina pattern, or a handprint.

- **Keypad/cipher lock**—These are convenient ways to control access without having to issue physical keys or access cards. The user must know the code to obtain access to the room or building.

- **Security guards**—Security guards are another form of physical controls, and should be trained on the policies and incident handling procedures to be followed.

Install and Configure a Basic Firewall—There are many types of firewalls, including the following:

- **Host-based**—Implemented in software on a specific computer or server.

- **Network-based**—Controls traffic that is attempting to cross the network. The firewall could be a physical or virtual appliance implemented in software as a virtual machine.

- **Application aware/context aware**—Can look higher than Layer 4 in the protocol stack. It makes decisions based on the applications that are being used at the application layer. It is sometimes referred to as a *context-aware firewall*.

- **Small office/home office**—Generally has many features of a corporate firewall but less capacity regarding throughput.

- **Stateful**—Analyzes outbound traffic and remembers those sessions by keeping that information in a stateful session table on the firewall. This is helpful when reply traffic comes back from the untrusted networks (the Internet). The firewall can dynamically recognize the return traffic and allow it. Stateful firewalls can also use access control lists (ACL).

- **Stateless**—Does not maintain the state information regarding sessions, but is more likely to make decisions based on a static access control lists that identify what traffic should be explicitly permitted or denied.

- **UTM (unified threat management)**—Includes a new generation of firewalls that consist of multiple features in one device. This can include the following:

  - Context-aware application inspection

  - Stateful filtering

  - Anti-malware protection

  - Antivirus protection

  - Data loss prevention, by looking for sensitive information such as Social Security numbers and preventing that information from leaving the network

  - URL filtering to prevent access to sites that are known to be inappropriate or unauthorized

- **Routed**—Appears and operates as a Layer 3 device.

A firewall can also be implemented in the network as a Layer 2 device, which is often referred to as *transparent* or *virtual wire* mode. Even though there is a Layer 3 routed interface on the firewall, it can still implement security policies at multiple layers of the protocol stack, including the application layer if it is an application-aware firewall.

A demilitarized zone (DMZ) is a section of the network that is neither the inside trusted network nor the outside untrusted network. The DMZ is a location where servers are placed to make them accessible from outside untrusted networks (Internet).

For inbound traffic, ACLs are usually employed on a firewall to permit specific traffic to the servers and the DMZ. The general rule for a firewall is an implicit deny. The firewall can be configured to allow all traffic that's being sourced from the inside network and going out, which is referred to as *outbound traffic*, while at the same time inbound traffic would likely be denied by default. Exceptions to this include inbound traffic that is coming back to the users through a firewall that is performing stateful inspection, and is dynamically allowing the return traffic back in. Firewalls can be located in multiple places, including internal, external, and at the edge of networks.

Usually, a firewall is placed between untrusted networks (the Internet) and a company's private networks. If there is a turnover of personnel and a new administrator does not know the management IP address or the password required to manage the firewall, the new administrator might have to completely reset the firewall back to its factory settings, and then start fresh with a brand-new configuration.

Network Access Control (NAC) Models—These models include the following:

- **802.1x**—This protocol is employed to authenticate a user and a wireless or wired environment before giving them further access into the network.

- **Posture assessments**—This is the process of validating that certain software is present and running on a system before allowing that system to have access to the network. This is in addition to user authentication. It could also be looking for specific values in the registry of a Windows computer or certain files that are present on the file system. A common use of posture assessment is to verify that a virus scanning program is present and up to date. Other software, such as a host-based firewall, could also be searched for in the posture assessment and required before access is allowed.

- **Guest network**—This is often created and provided, especially wireless, for individuals who are not employees or authorized users but still might want to have network access to the Internet while at the company being visited. Creating a separate guest network and isolating it from the company private network increases security through isolation.

- **Persistent versus nonpersistent agents**—The process of posture assessment can be performed through an agent. An agent is a piece of software that runs on the computer that is attempting to get access to the network. An agent can be persistent, meaning it is installed on the computer and is running all the time. An agent also might be nonpersistent, running only at the time of the assessment check, in which case after the assessment check is over the agent is no longer running in memory.

- **Quarantine network**—If a computer that is going through the posture assessment does not meet the requirements, it can be placed dynamically into a special VLAN or subnet that has the resources to allow the computer to be updated. Revisions can include file sharers with updated virus scanning tools or an updated host-based firewall. This special VLAN or network can also be referred to as a *remediation network*. After a user has performed the appropriate updates, the user can attempt to reauthenticate and go to the posture assessment to gain access to the network.

- **Edge and access control**—By implementing controls at the edge of the network, such as 802.1x and posture assessment, you prevent devices from accessing the network without the proper software or permissions. This is an example of controlling access to the network at the edge. After the user has been authenticated and connected to the network, you can further control access with ACLs and various permissions.

Basic Forensic Concepts—Procedures should be established in case of a security breach. The procedures may include these:

- **Designate a first responder**—This individual has been trained in procedures for dealing with an incident, including a security breach.

- Secure the area

- Escalate when necessary

- Document the scene

- Perform discovery

- Collect evidence/data—Make a complete replica or copy of a hard drive without changing or modifying even one bit of data on the original drive, to keep evidence intact. Hashes could be generated against the original and copied drives to verify data integrity. A matching hash represents that the copy is an exact replica.

- Document a chain of custody—Evidence should be tracked and documented from the moment it was discovered until it is being presented. If the chain of custody is lacking, gaps can provide an opportunity for tampering of evidence. Gaps in the chain of custody could also cause evidence to not be admissible in court.

- Document data transport

- Provide a forensics report—This identifies what was found, as well as the detailed steps that were used to acquire, analyze, and transport the data.

- Legal hold—This is the process that a company would follow to preserve all the evidence and relevant information when litigation is expected.

Chapter 18
Network Troubleshooting Methodologies

A well-thought-out troubleshooting methodology will assist you with networks that you are familiar with, as well as networks that you have recently been asked to work on. This chapter examines troubleshooting methodologies as presented in the CompTIA Network+ blueprint.

Identify the Problem—This is one of the first steps to solving any problem. Gather all the available information regarding the problem. If possible, try to duplicate the problem. Part of the investigation might involve questioning users regarding the symptoms. Pay specific attention to the symptoms users are experiencing as opposed to what a user believes the problem is. A user might not have enough technical knowledge to correctly diagnose the issue. After symptoms have been identified, determine whether anything has changed. For example, if a user cannot print today but could yesterday, and an update or an upgrade was performed overnight, that could be a reason for the failure of the printer today. If there are multiple problems, focus on each problem individually.

Establish a Theory of Probable Cause—The next step is to establish a theory of probable cause. This might involve questioning the obvious, as well as considering multiple approaches. Use a top-to-bottom approach from a protocol stack perspective. Check to see whether application layer services work; for example, check to see whether a client can access a web server over the network. Another approach is a bottom to top with respect to the protocol stack. Use this method to check the network interface card and cabling as a first step. Another option is to divide and conquer. An example would be using a traceroute or tracert to verify connectivity to the network, without using an application layer service. This divide-and-conquer approach might identify the location of the failures.

Test the Theory to Determine Cause—Test the theory to determine the cause of the problem. If the theory has been confirmed, identify the next steps to resolve the problem. If, in testing, a theory is not confirmed as being the problem, reestablish a new theory or escalate the problem if necessary.

Establish a Plan of Action to Resolve the Problem and Identify Potential Effects—One of the objectives in implementing a solution is to avoid creating any negative impact on the network. For example, if you make a router configuration change that solves the initial problem but then denies access for other applications that should be available, that is not an optimal resolution to the initial problem. A plan of action might also involve a formal change control process that identifies the actions or changes that are to be made, a rollback procedure if those changes are not successful, and proper authorization from management regarding the change that is proposed.

Implement the Solution or Escalate as Necessary—If the solution can be performed by you or your team, and presuming that the proper change control has been authorized, then the solution should be implemented. If the device to be configured or modified is managed by a different team, such as the firewall team, then the recommendation to implement a solution should be escalated to that team.

Verify Full System Functionality and, If Applicable, Implement Preventive Measures—After the solution has been implemented, testing should be done to verify full system functionality and security. For example, if an access control list was preventing functionality, the complete removal of that access control list might allow functionality but at the same time introduce a security risk. Steps should also be taken to help reduce the chance of the same problem happening again in the future. For example, if a user changed his own IP address on his computer, and that caused the failure, restrictions might be implemented to prevent the user from being able to tamper with the IP configurations on his computer in the future.

Document Findings, Actions, and Outcomes—Clear and accurate documentation and regular audits can keep management informed about the status of the network. Having documentation stored electronically provides access, over the network, to technicians, engineers, and help-desk personnel. Documentation should include findings, actions, and outcomes regarding the troubleshooting. Current network diagrams and topologies can also assist in making network troubleshooting more effective.

Chapter 19
Network Troubleshooting Tools

Many tools are available for troubleshooting networks. This chapter examines several tools that can be used from the command-line interface (CLI) of network devices, as well as physical and software-based troubleshooting tools.

Command-Line Tools

You might just fall in love with some of these command-line tools when it comes to troubleshooting your network. They are very quick and easy to use after you get some experience with them.

ipconfig—This command, which is part of most Windows operating systems, can be used to view the current IP protocol configuration on a Windows host. This could include details such as the IPv4 and IPv6 addresses, the default gateway, the DNS server, and the Layer 2 address of the Ethernet network interface cards. Table 19-1 shows the options for ipconfig.

Table 19-1   ipconfig *Options*

ipconfig Options	Function
/all	Provides details such as DNS and the Layer 2 MAC address for Ethernet interfaces
/release	Releases a DHCP lease
/renew	Renews a DHCP lease

netstat—This command can be used on Windows and Linux operating systems. The output of this command, based on the options used, can provide the details for incoming and outgoing network connections, routing tables, and open ports. Table 19-2 shows some commonly used options with the command.

Table 19-2   netstat *Options*

netstat Options	Function
-a	Shows the PC's active IP-based sessions
-r	Displays the PC's IP routing table

ifconfig—This command is integrated into most versions of Linux and UNIX operating systems and can also be found in Apple's OS X operating system. It shows the IP address configured on the host, as well as the details about the network interfaces.

ping/ping6/ping -6—The ping utility, which has versions to support both IPv4 and IPv6, can be used to verify Layer 3 connectivity between two networked devices. Behind the scenes, ping uses Internet Control Message Protocol (ICMP) to implement the network connectivity test.

tracert/tracert -6/traceroute6/traceroute -6—Traceroute and its variants display the path that a packet is taking as it goes over a network. The path indicates which Layer 3 devices (referring to IP routing devices) the packet is crossing to get to its final destination. The implementation of this command and the actual syntax vary based on the platform it's being used on. On some computers, such as Windows, the command is **tracert**. On other platforms, such as a Cisco IOS router, the command is **traceroute**.

In either case, the command is used in combination with a destination IP address regarding the path you want to see in the output of this command. Behind the scenes this command uses a feature called *time to live* (TTL), which is part of the IP header, to facilitate responses from each of the routers in the path to the final destination.

nbtstat—This command is used in many versions of Windows and can show details regarding Microsoft's NetBIOS, including name resolution. Name resolution in a Microsoft legacy environment could use a local file named LMHOSTS or a centralized Windows Internet name server (WINS) for the resolution of NetBIOS names to

IP addresses. This process is separate and could be used in addition to the DNS process that also performs name resolution for names to IP addresses.

nslookup—This tool is used for troubleshooting DNS name resolution. If a DNS problem is suspected, **nslookup** can be employed to verify whether the name resolution, using a specific DNS server, is working correctly.

arp—The **arp** command is used to see the local ARP cache on a host. This is important when troubleshooting to determine whether the Layer 3 to Layer 2 resolution is working correctly on an Ethernet network. Table 19-3 shows some common options used with the **arp** command.

Table 19-3 arp *Options*

ARP options	Function
-a	Displays current entries in a PC's ARP table
-d	Deletes an ARP entry for a host
-s	Statically adds a host entry in the ARP table

MAC Address Lookup Table—On a Layer 2 switch, the switch dynamically learns the MAC addresses of the devices connected to each of the switch's ports. You can look at the MAC address table on a Layer 2 switch in troubleshooting to see whether a frame from a computer or device has been seen by the switch. If the Layer 2 address of a host has not been learned by the switch, it could indicate there is a problem with the host, its network card, or the cabling that connects the host to the switch. It could also indicate an issue with the Layer 2 switch port itself.

pathping—This command provides the verification of Layer 3 connectivity between two devices on the network. It also offers path information similar to **traceroute** regarding the Layer 3 routers in that path.

Additional Troubleshooting Tools

In addition to the command-line tools just discussed, there are separate tools that can be used as part of troubleshooting network problems. This section takes a look at several of them.

Line Testers—Many types of lines are used in networks. These include phone lines, wide area network circuits, lines for closed-circuit television, and others. A line tester is a device that verifies whether a line is working correctly. It can confirm that specific voltages are present and that resistance or capacitance, or other characteristics, are in place that indicate that the line is suitable for its intended use.

Certifiers—These are devices that provide certification for network cables. A certifier can also represent the individual or company that is using the tools to certify cabling. A common example would be a cable tester that verifies the qualities of a cable to certify that the cable meets the specifications required by the technology being used, such as certifying a Cat 6 cable that is run from the patch panel in the wiring closet all the way to the RJ-45 wall jack in the user's office.

Multimeter—This is a device that has the capability to measure multiple electrical characteristics, including voltages, current, and resistance. A multimeter can be used in troubleshooting the power outlet in the user's office or to verify connectivity between pin 1 on one end of a patch cable and pin 1 on the other end.

Cable Tester—This is used to verify, troubleshoot, and, with the right equipment, certify a cable to be within certain specifications. A cable tester can be used to identify the lack of connectivity where it is expected, which is referred to as an *open*. It also recognizes when connectivity is present but shouldn't be. This is referred to as a *short*. A cable that is terminated incorrectly is likely to report some open connections as well as some shorted connections.

Light Meter—When used in the context of networking and fiber-optic cables, a light meter is used to troubleshoot a problem with a fiber-optic cable. There are specifications and limits regarding how much a fiber-optic cable can be bent, as well as the distance the fiber-optic signals are expected to travel and still be useful. A light meter, such as an optical time domain reflectometer (OTDR), helps identify issues in a fiber-optic cable run.

Toner Probe—This is very useful when it is not clear which cable or cables in the user's office terminate at which connections in the wiring closet. When a tone generator is connected to the wires in the user's office, a toner probe can be taken to the wiring closet and be used to individually touch different wires until a sound is heard. The sound indicates that the wire being touched with the toner probe connects to the wires in the user's office where the tone generator (which is part of the toner probe set) is connected.

Speed Test Sites—Building a baseline of what normal traffic looks like, which could include the identification of normal speeds during various times of the day, is useful as a comparison when the network seems slow. Many speed test sites are publicly available on the Internet. They provide a benchmark of throughput from the computer running the speed test to the Internet resource that is being used as part of that speed test.

Looking Glass Sites—These allow a glimpse into the network from a different perspective. For example, if you want to look at connectivity through your own network, you could use your own network devices with the appropriate show commands to see the details. A looking glass that is offered by a service provider on the Internet allows insight into the routing and paths that are being used on that service provider's network. A combination of this information and that of your own local network gives you a more accurate picture.

Wi-Fi Analyzer—This helps you to identify issues in which multiple access points are using overlapping channels, which are interfering with each other. A Wi-Fi analyzer could also indicate that a technology is being used other than the one that's intended. When a site survey is being performed for a wireless network, it is likely that a Wi-Fi analyzer would also be used to identify signal strengths, frequencies, and ranges that will work optimally in that space.

Protocol Analyzer—This is used to decode traffic that has been captured from the network. It examines the details regarding individual layers of a protocol stack, such as the TCP/IP protocol stack. When it's used for troubleshooting, issues such as malformed packets, nonresponding devices (such as a server that did not respond to a client request), and other problems could potentially be identified.

Chapter 20
Troubleshooting Wireless and Copper

This chapter addresses several issues that could impact network connectivity for network devices that are using wireless as well as physical cabling such as unshielded twisted pair (UTP) that uses copper.

Wireless Troubleshooting

This section focuses on issues related to troubleshooting wireless networks.

Signal Loss—Because wireless networks rely on wireless signals, a loss of signal is going to negatively impact that networked device. Signal loss can be caused by a lack of power to the access point or obstruction between the access point and the network device. A metal wall or a concrete wall would degrade the wireless signal. To prevent loss, ensure that the access point provides the desired coverage and there's nothing obstructing the signal between the user and the access point.

Interference—Radio frequency interference (RFI) can cause poor network performance or completely block it. Interference can be caused by other wireless devices that might be using the same frequency ranges as those used by the access points in your wireless network. Other nonnetwork devices, such as consumer-grade baby monitors or wireless telephones, can also interfere with wireless network signals.

Interference is also caused by access points that have overlapping coverage which are also using overlapping channels. Use a Wi-Fi analyzer to identify interference, and then resolve this issue by using nonoverlapping channels or other frequency ranges where there is less interference by other devices.

Overlapping Channels—In the 2.4 GHz range, the nonoverlapping channels in the U.S. are channels 1, 6, and 11. If there is a mismatched channel configuration such that two access points that are within range of each other are also using the same channel, it could cause interference between the two access points. Configuration should be done to ensure that access points that are within range of each other are using nonoverlapping channels.

Signal-to-Noise Ratio—In networking, the signal carries the desired information over the network. This concept applies to wireless as well as wired networking. Noise is additional information that is present on the network but is not part of the desired signal. If the signal-to-noise ratio is not good enough, meaning there is so much noise that the signal cannot be interpreted, it can lead to poor network performance. Analysis tools can monitor the signal-to-noise ratio. A solution for a poor signal-to-noise ratio is to move to frequencies that will have less noise, or move the access point and client closer together for an improved signal.

Device Saturation—*Saturation* refers to the density of devices, such as wireless clients, that are all using an access point. If the device saturation is too high, such as in a school environment or another public area, a single access point might not be able to carry the load for all users sufficiently. To correct this, additional access points should be implemented and users distributed among those multiple access points.

Bandwidth Saturation—This refers to all the bandwidth being used. On older wireless technologies a few users who are doing significant uploads or downloads could potentially utilize all the bandwidth available with the access point. A solution to this would be to use a larger bandwidth device or multiple ranges, as well as newer technologies that can support additional throughput.

Untested Updates—All new updates, such as patches, fixes, or upgrades, should be fully tested in a lab or test environment before being deployed in a production network. Having a test environment helps alleviate network downtime due to an update or patch causing a performance or security issue in the production network. The intention is that in a test or lab environment the updates can be tested and verified and checked for vulnerabilities before deployment on the production network.

Wrong SSID (Service Set Identifier)—Wireless devices often remember the wireless networks to which they have connected in the past. The benefit of this is that a wireless client can reconnect to a wireless network without requiring additional user intervention. If a user connects to an incorrect SSID in a production network, she might be putting her machine at risk. An example is a user who connects to a rogue or malicious access point, and as a result connects to an attacker's network. Any network shares where resources appear, if used by the wireless clients, might compromise that wireless client's computer. To prevent this problem from occurring, make sure that users can identify when they have connected to an unauthorized access point, how to protect against it, and how to report it.

Power Levels—The power levels of the access points must be within the regulated levels based on the country or principality where the wireless network is being used. In some cases, you might want to reduce the power level to prevent an access point from overlapping with another access point that might be using the same frequency ranges. Another example is to avoid sending wireless signals into an area where the wireless network is not needed, such as another office or parking area on the other side of the wall in the next building.

Open Networks—These are wireless networks that don't require authentication. They should be avoided because they pose a security risk. User authentication should be required on all corporate wireless networks. User awareness training should be done so that users know that they should not connect wireless devices (that might either contain company information or have connectivity to company resources) to open networks.

Rogue Access Point—This is a malicious access point that is not authorized to be used in the wireless space at your company. A rogue access point could use a similar or even the same SSID as the corporate wireless network, as an attempt to entice users to connect. When users are connected to a malicious or rogue access point, confidentiality can be compromised. The person managing the rogue access point could have direct access to all network traffic that is then going to or from the clients' wireless computers.

Wrong Antenna Type—Several types of antennas can be used with wireless networking. An omnidirectional antenna is a good choice for an access point that has a centralized location, where users are fairly evenly distributed within the range of that access point. A unidirectional antenna is beneficial when transmitting and receiving must be performed in a specific direction. If an incorrect antenna type is used, it could impact the signals and as a result the effectiveness of the wireless network.

Incompatibilities—Compatible wireless networking devices are critical for successful wireless networking. If the access point is configured to use only 802.11ac and the client is configured to use only 802.11b, that incompatibility will cause a failure between the access point and the client. In short, any features that are required for network connectivity on the wireless network must be supported by both the client and the access point. The distance covered by an access point should also be considered.

Wrong Encryption—Security for wireless networks is important. Having incompatible encryption capabilities could cause wireless failure. If the access point is configured to use only Advanced Encryption Standard (AES) while the client is configured to use only Wired Equivalent Privacy (WEP), the wireless client might not connect to the access point. The solution is to use the same type of encryption and security for the access point and the client.

Bounce—Wireless signals bounce off walls, ceilings, and other objects. Some technologies, such as 802.11n and 802.11ac, can leverage this tendency to some degree, but fewer obstructions between the access point and the client make for a better wireless connection. Obstructions should be removed if possible if they are causing network problems. Another option is to move the client or access point so that the obstructions are not causing any failures.

MIMO (Multiple Input Multiple Output)—This is a method used by both 802.11n and 802.11ac. It involves the use of multiple antennas and channels working simultaneously. If throughput is not as expected, verify that both the client and the access point have a strong enough signal between them. Also confirm that the client and access point both support the technology that uses MIMO, or in the case of 802.11ac, the enhanced multi-user MIMO (MU-MIMO).

AP (Access Point) Placement—This should be planned when the wireless site survey is being performed. The placement of the AP should allow adequate wireless coverage to all the clients that will use the access points for wireless access. The correct type of antenna should also be implemented to provide the expected coverage by each of the access points.

AP Configurations—Access points can be managed individually. When set up to be configured and managed separately, the access point is referred to as an *autonomous access* point, or a *thick access* point. When it's configured as an autonomous access point, the details regarding the technology to use, the signal strength, the speed and duplex for the wired connection to the switch, and the wireless frequency range to use are all configured and controlled locally at the access point.

An alternative to using the access points as autonomous APs is to employ them as a thin AP. A thin AP is configured to work with a wireless LAN controller (WLC). With a WLC, the administrator specifies details for the wireless network, and then the controller makes the individual implementations on the access points. As a result, the administrator must perforam a very thin or small configuration on the APs to initially associate an access point with the controller. After that, the controller provides the configuration details for each access point. A protocol used between a controller and an access point is Lightweight Access Point Protocol (LWAPP). In a Cisco Systems environment the protocol used between a controller and an access point is Control and Provisioning of Wireless Access Points (CAPWAP).

Environmental Factors—Concrete walls, window film, filing cabinets, or other obstructions between the access point and a wireless client can impact performance of the wireless network. This could also include material in the walls such as metal studs.

Wireless Standard Related Issues—When wireless standards are not followed, it can impact your expected results from the wireless network. This includes attempting to send more data than possible regarding a specific technology, or going farther than the distance supported, or using channels or frequencies outside the scope or specifications of a given technology. When in doubt, stay within the standards.

Copper Troubleshooting

Copper cabling often provides more reliable communications than wireless networking. Physical cabling is not using unlicensed radio frequencies that could be in competition with other companies' or individuals' access points. Other benefits of copper cabling include unshielded twisted pair, and the throughput is often greater using the Ethernet technologies compared to Wi-Fi. There are still plenty of things that can go wrong with copper cabling. This section addresses troubleshooting several of these possible issues.

Shorts—A short is when there is an unexpected connection. As an example, a straight-through Cat 6 UTP cable, which is terminated using RJ-45 connectors, should have pin 1 on one end of the cable that provides connectivity to pin 1 on the other end of the cable. If, when a cable tester is used, it is identified that pin 1 connects to pin 2, that is considered a short, as in a short circuit. It can be caused by an incorrect termination at one or both ends of the cable. The resolution is retermination of one or both ends of the cable using the standards.

Opens—An open is when there is a lack of connectivity. In a straight-through cable pin 1 should connect to pin 1 on both ends of the cable. If there is no connectivity, a cable tester shows this as an open. This should be fixed using a termination of one or both sides following the standards.

Incorrect Termination (Mismatched Standards)—There are two standards for the termination of RJ-45 with unshielded twisted pair. One is 568A and the other is 568B. For a straight-through cable terminate both sides following the 568A standard.

However, if one end is terminated using 568A, and the other end of that same cable is terminated using 568B, the resulting cable is a crossover cable. This can be used when connecting two like devices, such as two switches that are directly connected to each other. A straight-through cable is used when network devices such as computers, printers, and servers are connecting to a switch.

Crosstalk—Unshielded twisted pair has specific numbers of twists per foot per pair. The standards for unshielded twisted pair cabling also use specific wires from specific pairs for transmitting and receiving signals. When signals are sent over copper, a magnetic field is generated, which could cause leakage of the signals into other wires. This leaking of the signals between wires is referred to as *crosstalk*.

When measuring for crosstalk, a tester can look for near-end or far-end crosstalk. Near-end crosstalk occurs near the testing device, at the near end of the cable, and far-end crosstalk happens at the end of cable from the perspective of where the tester is being used. To counteract crosstalk, unshielded twisted pair uses the twists as a countermeasure. Correct pins and wires in the creek cabling must be implemented for Ethernet networks when you are using unshielded twisted pair.

EMI (Electromagnetic Interference)/RFI (Radio Frequency Interference)—EMI can disrupt the signals in copper cabling. The interference could place the signal-to-noise ratio in such a manner that the network might be unusable. An electrical motor that uses a high amount of current is also likely to generate a large magnetic field, which could cause electromagnetic interference if the unshielded twisted pair is too close to the motor. Use cable trays and cable management systems to keep unshielded twisted pair at a safe distance from large industrial motors or other causes of electromagnetic interference. Fiber-optic cabling is not susceptible to electromagnetic interference because it is not using any copper or conductive material in the cabling and uses light for signaling.

RFI is usually a concern when working with wireless networks. RFI could be caused by any device that is generating radio frequency that is conflicting with the frequencies that you are using for wireless networks. Use wireless analysis tools to identify the problem, and then resolve the problem by either moving to different frequencies for the wireless network or removing the source of the RFI when possible.

Distance Limitations—Pushing the limits for Ethernet cabling might work occasionally, but it is not worth the risk. Staying within the limits for distance and cabling specifications is critical to maintain a solid Layer 1 infrastructure. To resolve distance limitations, use technologies that can go farther, such as fiber optics, or place additional network devices closer to the client or server that needs the connectivity. An example of this is placing an additional switch that would allow another 100 m of connectivity from the switch to the client or server that needs that connectivity.

Attenuation/Decibel Loss—Attenuation and the loss of signal that is measured in decibels is a fact of life. If a situation occurs in which a client is getting degraded network access because of an Ethernet cable being too long (beyond the standards for that technology), the solution is to stay within the specifications. There will always be attenuation and signal loss for both wireless and wired networks, and staying within the specifications can resolve those problems.

Bad Connector—A bad connector or termination can be identified with a cable testing tool, and can be resolved by reterminating the cable using the standard pinouts and the correct connector.

Bad Wiring—This is identified using a cable tester and should be replaced using the category of cable, such as Cat 5 or Cat 6, based on the technology that you are using. Also be sure that the correct termination is used for the wiring or cabling being replaced.

Split Pairs—The unshielded twisted pairs have a specific number of twists per foot to minimize crosstalk, and specific wires from those pairs are used in networks. By following the standards for both the cable and the termination of those cables, you will avoid split pairs. A split pair is when the incorrect wires from the UTP are being used, and a single wire from one pair is used with a single wire from a different pair for the send or receive pins being used. Although you could still have a straight-through cable using split pairs, a cable tester could indicate that split pairs are in use because of the crosstalk that is present due to the split pairs. The resolution for this is to reterminate both ends of the cable using the standards, which use the correct wires and pairs for the sending and receiving of data.

Tx/Rx Reverse—If the transmit and receive connections are incorrectly terminated, it could lead to a connection failure between a host on the network and the switch. If the standards are followed for the termination of both ends of the cable, and the right type of cable, this problem can be avoided. A cable tester indicates that the transmit and receive wires are reversed, and retermination of the cable will correct the problem.

Cable Placement—Proper placement, especially for unshielded twisted pair, should be done to avoid being near sources of electromagnetic interference. Cable management, including the use of cable trays, protects the cables from physical abuse as well, such as being stepped on, tripped over, or stressed due to pulling. Appropriate cable placement along with proper labeling and documentation or patch panels and wiring closet connections improve the ability to troubleshoot if a connectivity issue is found.

Bad SFP (Small Form-Factor Pluggable)/GBIC (Gigabit Interface Converter)—SFP and GBIC are both examples of adapters that could be put into a switch port (for that type of adapter) that enable the switch to connect to certain types of cabling. These adapters act as transmitters and transceivers that work with specific types of cabling and connectors. For example, if you were using gigabit Ethernet on an older switch, you could purchase a GBIC that would plug in to the switch, and then from the GBIC it would connect to terminated Ethernet cabling. An SFP could be used to support Ethernet, including specific types of fiber-optic cabling and its termination (such as LC connectors for the fiber). If the incorrect type of SFP, GBIC, cable, or cable termination is used, it could cause a failure. A faulty or bad SFP, GBIC, cable, or cable termination can also cause a problem. Cable testers could be used on the physical cabling to verify and certify the cabling. Vendor-specific commands can be used on the switch to look at the details regarding the adapter that's plugged in to the switch. If a failure is found, or a problem is indicated, the offending adapter should be replaced to resolve the problem.

Chapter 21
Other Troubleshooting Areas

This chapter addresses several troubleshooting areas, some of which reinforce what has been discussed in previous chapters. It also presents new insights on trouble-shooting problems that can occur on networks today.

Fiber Troubleshooting

Fiber optics provide an advantage over copper cabling for Ethernet in that fiber-optic cables can go farther and have higher capacity for throughput. They are not subject to radio frequency or electromagnetic interference because they don't use copper for cabling but instead use light signals for transmitting and receiving data. Most of the problems presented in this chapter can be avoided or resolved by simply following the standards.

Attenuation/Decibel Loss—If a cable is longer than the specification or technology for which it is being used, the natural attenuation and decibel loss of the signal can cause the network to have faults or be completely unusable. The correction is to apply repeaters or other methods of regenerating signals so that the signal transmission is performed within the specifications of the technology being used.

SFP (Small Form-Factor Pluggable)/GBIC (Gigabit Interface Converter)—When fiber optics are used, switches can have a generic port that supports a module such as an SFP or GBIC module or adapter. The adapter chosen should be the correct one for the type of fiber termination as well as the type of fiber cable that is in use. If the incorrect SFP module for the incorrect cable type or termination is used, it could result in a failure. The resolution is to verify the type of module required, as well as the type of fiber cable that should be in place—for example, multimode versus single mode. Also within these categories are additional specifications that should be checked and verified.

Bad SFP/GBIC—The SFP or GBIC module acts as a transmitter and receiver that the switch uses to communicate over the fiber or Ethernet cable. If this adapter is the incorrect type, it would cause a failure for the fiber connection. Using the vendor's **show** commands can reveal additional details regarding the module, including any failures that the module might be experiencing.

Wavelength Mismatch—The SFP, connectors, and cabling all must support the type of frequencies used over a fiber cable. If there is a mismatch among the module type, the cabling, and the termination being used, that could cause a failure. You should verify the vendor's specifications and then confirm that the correct cable type and module are being used.

Fiber Type Mismatch—There are several types of fiber cabling, including multimode and single mode, and many variants within each of those categories. Confirm the use of the correct type of fiber cabling by comparing the standards along with the vendor's requirements to make sure that the correct cabling is being used, as well as ensuring compatibility with the SFP, cable termination, and port.

Dirty Connectors—A dirty connector at the termination of the fiber-optic cabling could prevent the signals from being received or sent successfully over the fiber-optic cable. The fiber-optic cable itself might be the problem. Verify this by using a fiber-optic cable tester, and have the termination cleaned if found to be dirty. The SFP adapter could be swapped out as part of a troubleshooting process and then the fiber cable could be reconnected to correct the problem.

Connector Mismatch—SFP modules are designed for specific fiber-optic termination, as well as specific frequency types to be used over the fiber cabling. Certain types of cabling are designed for different types of connectors. If not all of these items are compatible, it could cause a failure of the fiber optics. The resolution is to check all the specifications, and correct any components that are incompatible with the type of cabling or the technology being used.

Bend Radius Limitations—Fiber-optic cabling can be bent, to the extent that is planned for and documented as part of the specification (or recommendation) for that cabling. If the cable is bent in excess of the bend radius standards for fiber-optic cabling, the optical signal might not perform as well. There is also potential for permanent damage of the fiber due to causing miniature cracks in the cable. To help mitigate the potential of cables being harmed, cable management including the use of cable trays should be used. They can help keep the cables organized and protected against excessive bending.

Distance Limitations—Going beyond the distance of a standard, whether it be wireless, copper-based wire, or fiber-optic cabling, puts the network at risk. Failures are more likely to occur. Cable testers, including those specific for fiber optics, can be used to verify cabling plants including the distance of a fiber-optic cable. If a cable is found to extend farther than is supported by the technology, it should be modified or replaced within specs.

Common Network Issues

Many common issues can cause network failures or performance degradation. This section addresses them and what can be done to prevent or correct the network issues.

Incorrect IP Configuration/Default Gateway—A computer on an IP network needs a valid IP address to communicate with other devices on the same network and a default gateway to communicate with devices that are located on a different network or VLAN. To send packets back and forth to a remote network device, one or more routers operating at Layer 3 are used. A router on the local network of a computer can be used as a default gateway or default router. The default gateway can be learned and configured on a host using Dynamic Host Configuration Protocol (DHCP). The default gateway could also be statically configured on a computer along with its IP address and DNS server. If an incorrect default gateway is configured or supplied by a DHCP server, that would lead to the computer not being able to communicate with any devices that are outside its own local network. The resolution to this problem is to verify whether the computer has been configured with a default gateway that is on the same local subnet as the computer based on the computer's IP address.

Broadcast Storms/Switching Loop—A Layer 2 broadcast storm, which could be caused by a Layer 2 switching loop, is most likely caused by having two or more parallel paths between Layer 2 switches. To prevent broadcast storms and switching loops, Spanning Tree Protocol (STP) is used by the switches. If STP is disabled and there are parallel paths, it causes broadcast storms due to the switching loops. The resolution to this problem is to either remove the parallel paths so that there is only one path between the switches, or enable Spanning Tree Protocol, which dynamically identifies the parallel paths and prevents the switching loops from occurring by blocking one or more of the parallel paths.

Duplicate IP—On each IP network, host addresses must be unique (no duplicates). If manual configuration is being done for an IP address, it is possible that the same host IP address could accidentally be used on two different machines, which causes a problem. This is similar to having two houses on the same street with the exact same house number. When this occurs, most operating systems report either a pop-up message or a command-line message that there is a duplicate IP address in use on the network. The resolution to this problem is to identify the two computers that are using the same IP address, and change the IP address on one of them. To help identify the device or devices with the duplicate IP, ping can be used with the **arp -a** command to identify the Layer 2 address involved. After the Layer 2 addresses are identified, the MAC address table on the switch can be reviewed to distinguish which port the associated Layer 2 address is connected to.

Speed and Duplex Mismatch—Speed and duplex should both be correctly set up for optical network performance. Auto-negotiation often correctly negotiates the optimum speed that is compatible between the switch port and the device connected to that switch port. Duplex in a Layer 2 switch environment should always be full duplex. Using the appropriate **show** commands on the switch port reveals the current speed and duplex in use. At the computer that is connected to the switch port, the specific vendor operating system tools can be used to verify the speed and duplex. If one side is configured as half duplex and the other is full duplex, it results in poor performance for that network device when the network is busy. The correction is to configure the speed and duplex correctly on both the network device and a switch port. If auto-negotiation is not working correctly, those settings might need to be set manually.

End-to-End Connectivity—Testing end-to-end connectivity should be performed with a ping to a remote IP address. If the ping is not successful, a **traceroute** (or **tracert** if from Windows) can be done to identify the path or partial path that is being used to reach the destination. This helps identify the area in the network that is having routing problems. If the ping is successful but an application such as web services to the final destination is not, it can be because that application is not running on the destination host. Another reason might be an access control list on a router interface that is specifically prohibiting web traffic to the destination. The resolution is to identify where the fault is happening and then correct it. If a route is missing, a static route might need to be configured on a router or a dynamic routing protocol such as RIPv2 or OSPF might need to be configured so that the routers can dynamically learn all the routes in the network. If the issues are due to an access control list, the access control list might need to be changed or modified or reordered (meaning changing the order of the access list entries as they are processed from top to bottom) to allow the client to access the server using HTTP (Hypertext Transfer Protocol).

Incorrect VLAN Assignment—A switch port can be configured as an access port and associated with a single VLAN so that the client or device that is connected to the port is associated with that same VLAN. If the VLAN assignment on the switch port is incorrect, that could isolate the network device from being able to communicate with other devices on the network, including the default gateway. The solution for an incorrect VLAN assignment is to reconfigure the switch port to be associated with the correct VLAN.

Hardware Failure—This can occur on the network interface card of a computer or router, as well as a network interface port on a switch. If cabling is verified with a cable tester, hardware failure could be a possible reason for the network to not function for a specific device. An updated software driver or updated firmware software related to networking could also cause a problem. Updates should always be tested in a practice or test network before being used in production. If the hardware failure is on a common network device, such as a router interface, the impact would affect many users who are trying to use that router. If the hardware failure is on an end user's network interface card, it would impact only that user. The resolution is to identify where the failure is occurring and replace that hardware component. If the hardware component is integrated, such as a laptop or a switch port on a multiport switch, it might require replacing an entire unit to solve the problem. Another alternative is to simply use a different port when possible; for example, a user on a laptop could employ a network adapter that you can add to the system via USB.

Misconfigured DHCP (Dynamic Host Configuration Protocol)—A misconfigured DHCP server could hand out incorrect Internet protocol (IP), domain name service (DNS), and other DHCP options. Another possibility is that a misconfigured DHCP server might not hand out any IP address information at all. If hosts start by using an IPv4 address beginning with 169, that indicates that the computer was unable to obtain an IP address via DHCP, and it is using Automatic Private IP Addressing (APIPA) as a last resort. The resolution for a misconfigured DHCP server is to correctly configure the DHCP server. If the client is misconfigured to not use a DHCP server, due to being manually configured on the local computer, the resolution is to configure the PC to obtain an IP address automatically.

Misconfigured DNS—A DNS server that a host can use for name resolution can be obtained dynamically through DHCP, or it can be manually configured on the computer itself. If the DNS server is not reachable, or the DNS server IP address is incorrect and does not point to a real DNS server, that could cause a failure of name resolution on the PC. A tool such as **nslookup** can be used on a local computer to verify and test DNS name resolution. The correction to a misconfigured DNS server is to identify the problem, and then correct it by supplying a correct DNS server or allowing a host to be a DHCP client. By doing so, you dynamically learn the IP address of a correct DNS server.

Incorrect Interface/Interface Misconfiguration—Many configurations if done incorrectly could cause a network failure for a device or an entire network. The misconfiguration of an interface, or applying a configuration for the wrong interface, could cause problems. Examples of this include the wrong IP address on a Layer 3 interface, or the incorrect VLAN assignment on a switch port. To help correct these problems, care should be taken to verify the details that are being applied to an interface, as well as verifying that the correct interface is being configured.

Cable Placement—This should be performed by using cable management tools such as cable trays and patch panels. Appropriate wall jacks and correct documentation should also be used. Cable trays protect the cables from undesirable conditions, including electromagnetic interference, as well as physical abuse such as being bent or pulled on excessively, or being stepped on or tripped over.

Interface Errors—These are most likely visible on a switch port or router interface, compared to a user device. Such errors could indicate a problem with the interface, the devices sending signals back and forth over that interface, or the cabling being used to connect to the interface. Use monitoring tools such as SNMPv3 to securely allow events such as excessive interface errors to be reported to an SNMP management station. This station is where an alert is generated that enables an administrator or a technician to further investigate the errors. The resolution depends on the reason for the errors. If it is cabling, the cable should be corrected, which might involve the cable itself or the termination of the cable. If it is the device sending signals such as a host that is causing the problem, the resolution of the problem is performed on that device.

Simultaneous Wired/Wireless Connections—Many devices have more than one network interface card. For example, a laptop might have an RJ-45 connection for a wired network interface that is built in to the laptop, as well as a wireless network interface card that is also part of the laptop. If both interfaces are active and are connected to different networks, the operating system might not handle that situation successfully. This is due to being supplied IP addresses on two different networks, as well as default gateways on both networks that were learned via DHCP. One resolution for this is to disable one of the network interface cards. You can also use configuration tools that might be available as part of the operative system, or from a third party, to control network access and identify a priority regarding which network interface should be used if multiple networks are available.

Discovering Neighboring Devices/Nodes—Some devices on the network can use Layer 2 protocols for the dynamic discovery of other devices on the network. An example of this is Link Layer Discovery Protocol (LLDP). This is an open standard commonly used by vendors that create network gear, but it is not often implemented on end workstation devices. In Cisco, a proprietary Layer 2 discovery protocol named Cisco Discovery Protocol (CDP) is often used on Cisco devices for the dynamic discovery of neighboring Cisco devices and nodes, including switches, routers, and Cisco IP telephones. IPv6 has a protocol named Neighbor Discovery Protocol (NDP) that is used for neighbor discovery and many other IPv6-related functions. If there is a problem with neighbor discovery, verify that a common and supported discovery protocol is being used by all the devices that you want to be discovered.

Power Failure/Power Anomalies—Power, including sustained power at acceptable levels, is critical for networks. If there is a power failure or a power anomaly such as a brownout, sags, or dips, that can impact the network. To protect against this issue, use power conditioners with uninterruptible power supplies (UPS), which are battery backups. For longer-term protection against power loss, use power generators. One of the keys for managing power is to be proactive in identifying a problem, and reduce or negate the impact of the incoming issue on the network gear and devices that rely on the power.

MTU (Maximum Transmission Unit)/MTU Black Hole—MTU is the maximum size of a packet or frame that can be sent over a portion of a network. Some network devices, including routers that are routing packets, might need to send packets over a section of the network that supports a smaller MTU than the incoming original packet. Often, a router divides the original packet into two or more fragments to accommodate a smaller MTU before forwarding them. If a network device, such as a router, has a smaller MTU but is unable to fragment the packet and is also unwilling to reply to the sender to indicate that there is a problem, an MTU black hole will result. A solution to this issue is an application that does MTU discovery end to end between the sender and the receiver. This device discovers the maximum MTU supported, and then never exceeds that MTU during the network session.

Missing IP Routes—This is inadequate information. On a computer, a missing default route prevents the computer from sending packets outside its own local IP network. An unreachable default gateway—for example, a default gateway that is on a different subnet—is considered an unreachable default gateway. On a router, a missing route could mean the router is unable to forward a packet to a network. Using **traceroute**, as well as displaying the routing table, helps identify a missing IP route. The correction to this problem is to either add a static route or implement a dynamic routing protocol that enables the router to dynamically learn the routes it needs.

NIC (Network Interface Card) Teaming Misconfiguration—Vendors of network devices and servers often implement the feature of port bonding, or the linking of multiple interfaces into one logical interface. Other options include using multiple network interface cards on a server for fault tolerance, in which one interface is used primarily, and the other interface is used only if the primary card fails. This is often referred to as *NIC teaming*. If there is a misconfiguration of NIC teaming, it could cause a failure of one or both of the network interface cards. The resolution to this problem is to identify the correct requirements from the vendor regarding the types of cards, the configuration supported, and the switch port configuration (where the network interface cards connect to the switch) to make sure that the teaming is being implemented correctly.

Security Issues

Security is a double-edged sword. Without it, unauthorized access becomes easily available. Incorrectly configured security could also provide unauthorized access or prevent access by authorized users. This section identifies potential security issues and how to resolve them.

Misconfigured Firewall—A firewall's job is to restrict unauthorized access. There are many types of firewalls. One of the first things that should be done when implementing a firewall is to identify the policy that specifies what types of traffic, services, and users should be allowed access through the firewall. After that's identified, the rules and settings on that firewall should be applied to support that policy. A misconfigured firewall might include allowing all traffic from anyone to any service through the firewall, which would likely lead to a security breach. Another example of a misconfigured firewall is one that does not allow any traffic, including authorized users' traffic, to go through it. Correcting a firewall might include modifying access control lists or include a complete rebuild of the firewall configuration. If the username and password or the IP address for managing the firewall is unknown, it might require a factory reset of that firewall, which will then allow initial access to the CLI, and then the firewall can be configured starting from the factory configuration. The new configuration should correctly implement the company policy.

Misconfigured ACLs (Access Control List)/Applications—A misconfigured ACL might be too permissive and allow traffic that should otherwise be denied. Access control lists are generally processed as a list going from the top to the bottom. Reordering the access control list might be required to correct a problem in which an entry near the top of the list is denying traffic before another entry near the bottom of the list is processed. After there is a match between an IP packet and an entry of the access control list, an action is taken, such as permit or deny, and the rest of the list is not processed regarding that packet. Applications that are misconfigured might provide additional information, including unauthorized information that should otherwise not be provided.

Malware—This is malicious software that runs on a computing device, usually without the user's awareness or consent. Malware can be implemented by various methods, including the user opening an attachment to an e-mail message that is then run as an application, or by the user visiting the website and clicking on something that installed the malware. To protect against malware, users should be trained on security awareness, and anti-malware software should be running on computers to help protect against it. Network-based devices such as Intrusion Prevention Systems (IPS) and unified threat management systems (UTM) can also help protect against malware.

Denial of Service (DoS)—A DoS attack prevents services that should normally be available. Examples include an attack that disables the services of a server or prevents network communication due to an attack. Because there are so many types and methods for a DoS attack to occur, there is not one simple solution. Some approaches to mitigating a Denial of Service attack include hardening network devices, including routers and servers and hosts, by removing unneeded services and controlling what those devices are allowed to do. Another method includes throttling or controlling the amounts of certain types of traffic on a network. Using IPS and UTM devices can also assist in preventing DoS attacks from being successful. Keeping up to date on patches, specifically security updates, is also important. Any updates should be tested in a lab or test network before being applied, and implementation in production networks should be done through proper change control.

Open/Closed Ports—When services such as web, File Transfer Protocol (FTP), or instant messaging are running on a computer or server, the well-known server ports are waiting and listening on those devices. These are known as *open ports* that respond to requests sent to those ports. A closed port is a port number that is not accepting incoming requests or being used for communications by that computer. Open ports, especially for services that are not intended to be running, pose a security risk because an attacker can run a network scanning tool to identify open ports, and then proceed to leverage those open ports in the applications behind those open ports in an attempt to compromise the network.

ICMP (Internet Control Message Protocol) Related Issues—ICMP is used for many services in IP. By manipulating the use of ICMP and the protocols that use it, an attacker can compromise the network or cause a DoS attack. An example of one of the oldest types of ICMP abuse is called the *ping of death*, in which a ping request (which uses ICMP) is sent with an extremely large size. The device receiving that request cannot correctly handle this ping packet. This could cause a DoS by preventing the TCP/IP protocol stack on the destination device from working. Fortunately, most modern operating systems are no longer affected by the ping-of-death attack. ICMP is a very helpful protocol when not abused. For example, when **traceroute** is used (or **tracert** on Windows), it is an ICMP message that is being sent back by each of the routers in the path. It notifies you that those specific routers are in the path to a final destination. If a router is supposed to route a packet but cannot due to a missing route in the routing table or an access control list, it can use ICMP to send a message back to the source. This indicates that the packet was dropped. Often, the reason it was dropped is also part of the ICMP message the router sends back to the device that sent the original packet.

Unpatched Firmware/OSs—Security updates include software or firmware updates. These are delivered as major or minor updates, patches, or fixes. Before any patches or updates to software or firmware are performed on operating systems, they should be thoroughly tested in a lab or test environment to verify functionality as well as security. If there is a known security flaw and a security patch is available, it should be implemented as quickly as it can be tested and verified.

Malicious Users—A malicious user is a user who is either trusted (meaning the person has a user account and been granted access to the network at some level) or untrusted. In either case, a user could launch attacks against the network to discover details. Methods for discovery and reconnaissance include network scans and packet sniffing. If clear-text unsecure protocols such as HTTP, FTP, and Telnet are being used, and if usernames and passwords are being used with these protocols, the attacker could learn these credentials and passwords by using a protocol analyzer with the packet capture that was gathered via the packet sniffer.

Authentication Issues—The authentication of administrators is often done using a centralized TACACS+ server in a Cisco environment. TACACS+ is a Cisco proprietary AAA solution. When TACACS+ is used, there is a separate session for each of the authentication, authorization, and accounting functions. If a network device is unable to use a configured TACACS+ AAA server, troubleshooting might involve verifying that the password configured on both the AAA server and the network device that is trying to use the AAA server is correctly configured. For end-user authentication and authorization, it is common to use a centralized AAA server using Remote Authentication Dial-In User Service (RADIUS). If the network device is unable to communicate with a AAA server, troubleshooting might involve verifying network connectivity between a networked device and the AAA server using **ping** or **traceroute**. You might also verify the password that is configured on both the AAA server (in this case, a RADIUS AAA server) and the device that is trying to access the AAA server. Any new device that is deployed in a network should require at least the password before allowing access. For more security, a combination of username and password and possibly multifactor authentication might be required. Many vendors have equipment with a default password, which if not changed could be a vulnerability because an attacker could attempt to use that password for access to the network device.

Improper Access/Backdoor Access—Often when developing a system, a programmer might build in backdoor access that bypasses the normal security for the system. This is often done for the sole purpose of saving time during the development process. After the system is developed, any backdoor access, which is an example of improper access, should be removed for overall security purposes.

ARP (Address Resolution Protocol) Issues—ARP is the means by which a computer on an Ethernet network can dynamically discover the Layer 2 address of another device on that same IPv4 network. Unfortunately, an attacker who is connected to the same network can perform Layer 2 ARP spoofing, which places incorrect Layer 2 mappings in the ARP cache of other devices in that same network. This is also referred to as *ARP cache poisoning.* The intent of the attacker is to trick the network into forwarding frames to the attacker's Layer 2 address, which should normally be forwarded to a server or the default gateway. To reduce the risk of this type of an attack, switch security, including ARP inspection, can be implemented to stop the ARP spoofing and ARP cache poisoning.

Banner Grabbing/OUI (Organizational Unique Identifier)—Banner grabbing is a process an attacker uses to learn additional information about an end system or server based on how that server responds to requests. For example, an attacker might be able to discover that a web server is running a specific vendor's implementation of software. The attacker might then be able to further discover vulnerabilities with that web server version and exploit them.

Many vendors' products have embedded OUI as part of their devices, which can also provide information to an attacker regarding the type of network device or network interface card that is being used. To lessen the risk of banner grabbing or revealing information regarding OUI, firewall rules and policies should be implemented. This restricts specific information from being sent back to an attacker when the firewall is in the path between the attacker and the server.

Domain/Local Group Configurations—Microsoft's active directory networking provides the capability to do single sign-on (SSO). Single sign-on enables users to authenticate once and as a result receive access to the network devices and services that they are entitled to use. A popular way of managing active directory domains is through group management. Providing a group access to network resources, and then associating multiple user accounts with that group, simplifies administration. Besides domain groups that are systemwide, there are also local groups and individual Windows servers and computers. If the permissions granted in either the domain or the local groups are incorrect or are too lenient, this poses a security risk. Periodic auditing should look for user accounts that have not been used for an extended period, which can then be disabled or deleted. The individual rights that a user has received either directly or through group membership should also periodically be audited to verify that the user does not have excessive rights. Excessive rights occur when a user is assigned temporary job responsibilities that require receiving additional rights and group membership, and when the assignment is completed, they are not removed from those groups.

Jamming—This is a process of disrupting signals with the intention of making them unusable. If an attacker is performing jamming on a wireless network, it can be devastating for the entire wireless network. To reduce this risk, a wireless LAN controller that is managing a group of access points can report on both rogue access points and malicious activity. Some vendors can also implement jamming to prevent the signals of a rogue access point from successfully being used in the corporate network.

WAN Issues

This section discusses several wide area network (WAN) related issues and how to solve them.

Loss of Internet Connectivity—A branch office could be using the WAN connectivity to the corporate headquarters for access to the Internet as well as access to headquarters. For this to be successful, the branch router or routers should have a default route that forwards packets over the WAN link to the headquarters location. In addition, the headquarters location should have Network Address Translation (NAT) rules to translate traffic coming from the branch office before routing those packets out to the Internet. If the WAN connection fails to provide Internet access, tools like traceroute can be used to verify connectivity between the branch office and headquarters location, as part of the troubleshooting process. The solution to the loss of Internet connectivity depends on where the problem is. The issue could be at the branch router, the headquarters router, or the headquarters connection to the Internet through the service provider.

Interface Errors—The interfaces used on the routers for wide area network connectivity should not have excessive errors. The vendor-specific commands on the router can reveal the quantity of interface errors. This could be due to hardware errors on the interface or the cabling between the interface and the service provider's equipment, or signals that are out of spec that are being sent to the interface to the service provider connection.

Split Horizon—This is a routing rule that informs the router that it cannot advertise a network over the same interface that it learned about a network. An example of this would be a headquarters location with two branch offices. If the headquarters router is using one physical interface and one logical network for the WAN connectivity to reach both branch offices, if the first branch office advertises a network to headquarters office, the split-horizon rule prevents the headquarters office from advertising that route via a dynamic routing protocol to the second branch office. The result is that the second branch office does not receive the routing information that is being advertised by the first branch office. Effectively, there could be one or more missing routes from the routing tables on the routers as a result. To resolve this problem in some environments, the feature of split horizon is disabled on the specific WAN interfaces where split horizon is causing the problem.

DNS (Domain Name System) Issues—DNS issues regarding WAN connectivity are the same as they are for local area network (LAN) connectivity. If DNS is not configured properly, or if the DNS server is not reachable, name resolution can fail. When virtual private networks (VPN) are allowing remote access, the VPN clients are often informed of a DNS server that can be used that is internal to the network when resolving the IP address for specific domains such as Acme.com. In those situations, if the VPN tunnel is active for the remote clients and the client attempts to resolve anything ending with Acme.com, the DNS information provided to the VPN service is used. Name resolution for any other host names outside Acme.com can be accomplished through the remote client's normal Internet-based DNS server. This is an example of split DNS.

Interference—Interference of signals, whether they are wireless or going over copper medium, can degrade or even stop network connectivity. Use cable management to avoid sources of electromagnetic interference, and implement proper wireless site surveys to avoid radio frequency interference. If problems occur, tools such as cable testers and Wi-Fi analyzers can be used.

Router Configurations—Routers are a key component in network connectivity. Router configurations should be protected, and if changes are made, they should be performed by authorized administrators with proper change control. Tests should be performed in a practice or test environment before changes are implemented. Backups of router configurations should be stored periodically and available if the system needs to be restored due to a complete loss of a router. You might also use a backup simply for rolling back a previous configuration to the router before changes were made.

CPE (Customer Premise Equipment)—This is physical equipment that is at the customer's physical location. An example might be a multilayer switch that a service provider owns and has physically located at the customer site to provide the customers connectivity for WAN and Internet services. Care should be taken to protect against unauthorized access and changes to this equipment. Something as simple as powering off the switch or other customer premise equipment could cause a DoS regarding the connectivity that was delivered by the service provider.

The demarcation point, often referred to as the *demarc* or *point of demarcation* (POD), is the physical point where the public network from a service provider ends and the private network of a customer begins. This interface between the service provider and the company receiving WAN services is also sometimes referred to as a the *network interface unit* (NIU).

A smart jack, also known as an *intelligent network interface device* (INID), can be used as a connecting point between the company's network gear and the WAN circuits supplied by the provider. One of the benefits of a smart jack is that it usually includes circuits as well as connectors that can be used for diagnostics if there are problems.

A loopback, which for the WAN circuits might be a physical plug or might be logically implemented using an intelligent network interface device, allows for a service provider to test a circuit to verify its functionality. This can be very helpful in troubleshooting when all the configuration cables on the customer side seem to be correct, and the WAN link being provided by the service provider is suspected of not being functional.

A channel service unit/data service unit (CSU/DSU) is a device that converts the digital signals that are used by the customer's router interfaces to make the signals compatible with the signals used on the wide area network. Decades ago this might have been an external device that would connect to both the customer router and the wide area network circuit from the provider. In more modern implementations this functionality is built in to the network interface card that can directly connect to the wide area network circuit, such as a T1. When distances are longer than the specifications regarding signals over copper cabling, repeaters and/or copper line drivers are used to regenerate and amplify the signal to keep it at an acceptable level.

Company Security Policy—This policy should be created by senior management, and the details of the policy should be interpreted and implemented to enforce it. A company security policy could include the throttling or the limiting of certain types of traffic that could help protect against a DoS attack. Limiting specific types of traffic can also provide protection against leaking data that might be sensitive or confidential. A security policy also can indicate that certain types of websites should not be accessible from company computers. This type of URL filtering based on type is a form of blocking. Blocking can also be applied to certain types of inbound requests to public-facing servers to help protect against attacks targeting those servers. A corporate policy might also include details regarding fair access and utilization limits to protect against misuse of network resources and services, including Internet access.

Satellite Issues—Satellite connections are often used when no other faster WAN connectivity is available. One of the biggest challenges with satellite is latency, and the delay it takes for a signal to be sent up to a satellite. One solution for dealing with the delay and latency introduced by satellite communications is to avoid using real-time applications such as voice and video that require near-real-time interaction. Alternative WAN services, if available, should be selected. Applications such as e-mail that do not require low latency or delay can be used over satellite connections without the concern. Satellite communications are also generally going to be low bandwidth. As a result, you might want to apply traffic shaping and Quality of Service (QoS) so that the most critical traffic is forwarded first and the remaining traffic can be queued or occasionally dropped due to lack of bandwidth.

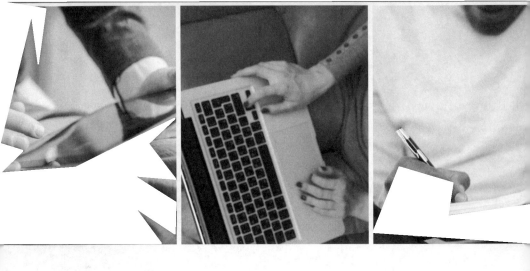

Chapter 22
Networking Standards

This chapter addresses many of the networking standards and theories that are used in computer networks, as well as the ports employed by many common applications. This chapter also contains policies and procedural concepts.

The OSI Model

This section discusses the Open Systems Interconnection model as a reference point that can be used to describe functionality in a computer network.

Layer 1—The physical layer, also known as Layer 1, deals with the transmission of bits over the network. This includes both copper and fiber cabling, as well as radio frequency when used as part of wireless networks. An unmanaged hub that is simply acting as a repeater is considered a Layer 1 device.

Layer 2—The data link layer, also known as Layer 2, is responsible for the packaging or encapsulation of packets into Layer 2 frames on an Ethernet network. As part of the frames, a new header is added that includes the source and destination Layer 2 MAC addresses on an Ethernet network. Network interface cards that support Ethernet have a built-in Layer 2 address, often referred to as the *MAC address* or the *physical address*. A device that makes forwarding decisions based on the Layer 2 addresses is known as a Layer 2 switch.

Layer 3—The network layer, also known as Layer 3, is responsible for forwarding packets based on their IP address. At Layer 3, header information is added, which includes the source and destination IP address for that packet. A device that makes forwarding decisions based on this Layer 3 information is known as a *router*. A device that has the capability to make Layer 2 forwarding decisions as well as Layer 3 forwarding decisions is referred to as a *multilayer switch*.

Layer 4—The transport layer, also known as Layer 4, receives data from the upper layer and encapsulates it using the Layer 4 protocol that is specified for the application data being carried. For example, for a customer who is using Hypertext Transfer Protocol (HTTP) for an application layer service, as that data is encapsulated at Layer 4, the Layer 4 protocol used would be Transmission Control Protocol (TCP). Port numbers are included in the Layer 4 header that indicate the upper-layer service or application that is being transported. Several protocols can be used at Layer 4, but the two primary protocols are TCP and User Datagram Protocol (UDP). TCP is connection-oriented and uses sequence numbers and acknowledgments. UDP is connectionless and does not use any synchronization or acknowledgments in its communications.

Layer 5—The session layer, known as Layer 5 in the OSI model, is responsible for setting up, maintaining, and tearing down sessions between devices.

Layer 6—The presentation layer, known as Layer 6, is responsible for the encryption and data formatting that is coming from the application layer.

Layer 7—The application layer, known as Layer 7, provides application layer services regarding network resources. In the current TCP/IP protocol suite there are not seven separate layers. Layers 5, 6, and 7 are all grouped together as one logical layer, and this is referred to as the *application layer*.

Network Theory

This section discusses various network theory concepts.

Encapsulation/De-encapsulation—Encapsulation is a logical process of manipulating data as it goes down a protocol stack. It begins with the application layer and works its way down to the physical layer. Part of the encapsulation process at the various layers includes providing additional information as part of a header.

As an example, when data is sent from the transport layer down to the network layer, the network layer takes the existing data, encapsulates it, and adds a brand-new header at Layer 3. This new Layer 3 header includes the additional information of source and destination IP address. As the Layer 3 packet is handed down to Layer 2, Layer 2 takes the existing information and encapsulates it again, adding its own Layer 2 header. The Layer 2 header can include the source and destination Layer 2 addresses, which on Ethernet are MAC addresses.

When a device on the network receives information, it performs de-encapsulation as the data moves up the protocol stack. An example is a web server that receives a frame of data. The web server looks at the Layer 2 destination address, and if that destination address matches the web server's own Layer 2 address, the web server removes the Layer 2 header and then analyzes the Layer 3 information.

The process of stripping away the header information as the data is analyzed higher and higher in the protocol stack is referred to as *de-encapsulation*. Upon looking at the Layer 3 information, if the web server determines that the destination IP address contained in the Layer 3 header is the web server's IP address, that causes the web server to continue to de-encapsulate that packet, at which point it disposes of the old Layer 3 information and continues to analyze at Layer 4. Encapsulation is the adding of information of various layers as data moves from the application layer down the protocol stack. De-encapsulation is the process of stripping off that additional header information at each of the levels as traffic moves up the protocol stack by the receiving device.

Modulation Techniques—There are several methods of encoding data so that it can be sent over the network.

Modulation of a waveform modifies one or more properties of a waveform to encode the data onto the carrier signal.

Multiplexing is a concept of integrating multiple streams of information at the same time. For example, there might be a single leased line connection between two offices, but when multiplexing is used, a portion of that leased line could be used for voice traffic and other portions of that leased line could be used for data traffic.

One example of a multiplexing method is to use time-division multiplexing (TDM). When individual time slots are associated with various network services, this method is used to share the bandwidth on a leased line between one or more applications or services that need use of that bandwidth. Another feature called statistical TDM can leverage the fact that not all the applications or services might need all the bandwidth that they are allocated all the time. As a result, statistical TDM allocates more time slots to applications or services that need them if at the same time the other services do not.

De-multiplexing is the process of separating the streams at the receiving side when the sending side has performed multiplexing.

Analog and digital signals can both be used to transmit data. This is done by converting the information into electrical signals. When analog technology is used, the data is converted into electrical pulses of varying amplitude. When digital is used, the data is sent in a binary format (either a 0 or a 1) and sent one bit at a time. With digital technology, one specific amplitude or voltage level could represent a one, and a different specific amplitude or voltage level could represent a zero.

Numbering Systems—The base-10 numbering system is referred to as *decimal*. It is likely that humans use the base-10 numbering system because we have ten digits, five on each hand. The ten unique numbers are 0–9. Computers and networks use a base-2 numbering system called *binary*. In a base-2 binary numbering system there are only two unique numbers, 0–1. Often you will use decimal to represent binary numbers. An example of this is representing an IPv4 address. The IPv4 address is really 32 binary bits, but you use decimal to represent it because decimal is easier to type and communicate.

Another numbering system is a base-16 system, called *hexadecimal*. In hexadecimal the range of numbers is 0–F, which is similar to the decimal until you go past 9, and then in hexadecimal it continues with A, B, C, D, E, and F. When working with IPv6 addresses, you represent them using hexadecimal, even though the IPv6 address is really a 128-bit binary number. There are other numbering systems as well, such as octal, which uses a base-8 numbering system.

Broadband/Baseband—This implies more than one signal or channel of data being sent at a time. Coaxial cable service from a cable company can deliver data, TV, and voice services over a single broadband cable connection. Baseband implies that only one single signal or channel can be used at a time. An example of baseband is a computer connected to a switch using unshielded twisted pair and running Fast Ethernet, also referred to as 100BASE-T. The keyword *base* in 100BASE-T represents baseband.

Bit Rate Versus Baud Rate—The bit rate is the number of data bits transmitted in one second. Baud rate refers to the number of times a signal in a communications channel changes. The baud rate, which represents data being communicated, is less than the bit rate.

Sampling Size—Sampling size refers to quantity. When data is being encoded on a network, the technology being used identifies the voltages and other electrical characteristics that represent data. The specifications also include details about sampling size, so both the sending and the receiving devices can correctly encode and decode the signals off of the network by using the same standard.

CSMA/CD (Carrier Sensing Multiple Access with Collision Detection) CSMA/CA (Carrier Sensing Multiple Access with Collision Avoidance)—CSMA/CD is an older Ethernet technology that was exclusively used before Layer 2 switches. A network device would listen to detect whether anyone else was communicating on the network, and would communicate only when there were no communications on the wires. If two devices attempted to communicate at the same time, they would both detect a collision. They would both back off, and after a random short period would attempt to communicate again if they sensed that the network was free.

CSMA/CA can include request-to-send and clear-to-send messages, which enable devices to coordinate their efforts and avoid collisions. Collision-avoidance mechanisms are still used in wireless networks today.

On local area networks that are using wired Ethernet with Layer 2 switches, you don't need collision detection or collision avoidance because each port on the switch is a dedicated path between the computer and the switch when you are in the common full-duplex configuration. The switch has a high-speed backplane and buffering capabilities to prevent collisions from happening anywhere in the switched infrastructure.

Wavelength—This is the distance between identical points in a waveform signal between two adjacent cycles of that waveform. When dealing with fiber optics, you can use different groupings of wavelengths as individual channels to send multiple sessions of data over a single fiber-optic cable.

TCP/IP Suite—The TCP/IP protocol suite is the primary protocol used today for both corporate networks and the Internet. The two main protocols at the transport layer in the TCP/IP protocol suite are TCP and UDP. The Internet Control Message Protocol (ICMP) is used as part of the TCP/IP protocol suite. An example of using ICMP is the **ping** command, which uses ICMP for the ping requests and replies.

Wireless Standards

Wireless standards, along with networked devices that follow them, allow for communications using radio frequency as the communications path.

802.11a—The 802.11a WLAN standard supports speeds as high as 54 Mbps. Other supported data rates are 6, 9, 12, 18, 24, 36, and 48 Mbps. The 802.11a standard uses the 5 GHz band and uses the orthogonal frequency-division multiplexing (OFDM) transmission method.

802.11b—The 802.11b WLAN standard supports speeds of 5.5 and 11 Mbps. The 802.11b standard uses the 2.4 GHz band and uses the Direct-Sequence Spread Spectrum (DSSS) transmission method.

802.11g—The 802.11g WLAN standard supports speeds as high as 54 Mbps. As with 802.11a, other supported data rates include 6, 9, 12, 18, 24, 36, and 48 Mbps. 802.11g works in the 2.4 GHz band, which enables it to offer backward compatibility to 802.11b devices. 802.11g can use either the OFDM or the DSSS transmission method.

802.11n—The 802.11n WLAN standard supports a wide variety of speeds, depending on its implementation. The speed of an 802.11n network could exceed 300 Mbps. 802.11n can operate in the 2.4 GHz band and/or the 5 GHz band. 802.11n uses the OFDM transmission method.

802.11n uses a technology called *multiple input multiple output* (MIMO) with multiple antennas. Channel bonding is also supported. With channel bonding, two wireless bands can be logically used together.

802.11ac—The 802.11ac WLAN standard builds on 802.11n. 802.11ac is a 5 GHz only technology and can use wider channels in the 5 GHz band, more spatial streams, and multi-user MIMO (MU-MIMO). 802.11ac with an 80 MHz channel width can support 433 Mbps per stream and multiple simultaneous streams.

Wired Standards

Standards for Ethernet over copper and fiber provide the details regarding media type, bandwidth capacity, and distance limitations as shown in Table 22-1. This section contains many of the common Ethernet standards.

Table 22-1 *Standards for Ethernet over Copper and Fiber*

Standard	Media Type	Bandwidth Capacity	Distance Limitation
10BASE-T	Copper Cat 3 (or higher) UTP	10 Mbps	100 m
100BASE-TX	Copper Cat 5 (or higher) UTP	100 Mbps	100 m
1000BASE-T	Copper Cat 5e (or higher) UTP	1 Gbps	100 m
1000BASE-TX	Copper Cat 6 (or higher) UTP	1 Gbps	100 m
10GBASE-T	Copper Cat 6a (or higher)	10 Gbps	100 m
100BASE-FX	Multimode fiber	100 Mbps	2 km
10BASE-2	Copper coaxial	10 Mbps	185 m
10GBASE-SR	Multimode fiber	10 Gbps	26–82 m
10GBASE-ER	Single-mode fiber	10 Gbps	40 km
10GBASE-SW	Multimode fiber	10 Gbps	300 m

IEEE 1905.1-2013—This is a standard for home networking for both wireless and wired technologies. It includes several details, including the possibility of using Ethernet over high-definition multimedia interface (HDMI) and Ethernet over power lines within a home.

EIA/TIA 568A/568B—This is a standard for how an RJ-45 connector should be terminated on a UTP cable. If both ends of the cable are terminated as 568A, the cable is a straight-through cable. If both ends of the cable are terminated using the 568B standard, the cable is once again a straight-through cable. If a crossover cable is desired, one end of the cable is terminated using 568A, and the other end is terminated using 568B.

The standards for which wires should be used with which pins on the RJ-45 connector are listed in Table 22-2 and Table 22-3.

Table 22-2 *T568A*

Pin #	Wire
1	White/green
2	Green
3	White/orange
4	Blue
5	White/blue

Pin #	Wire
6	Orange
7	White/brown
8	Brown

Table 22-3 *T568B*

Pin #	Wire
1	White/orange
2	Orange
3	White/green
4	Blue
5	White/blue
6	Green
7	White/brown
8	Brown/brown

DOCSIS (Data-Over-Cable Service Interface Specification)—DOCSIS is an international standard that enables the transmission of high-bandwidth data over an existing coaxial cable TV system. Users who receive network services from their cable providers are likely using a DOCSIS cable modem as part of the delivery for the services.

Policies and Procedures

Policies should be created by senior management and implemented to enforce the policies. This section addresses various elements of policies and procedures.

Security Policies—Part of a security policy should include the definition of what the critical assets are in the company, both physical and intellectual, and should specify how those resources should be protected. Policy users of the system might be required to consent to monitoring. This means that users are aware that these monitoring activities are present and they consent to having their actions and activities recorded as part of the use on that system.

Network Policies—Network policies can include the types of content and data to be accessed and used over the network. For example, a network policy might specify that certain types of websites should not be accessed. The enforcement of the policy could be implemented using firewalls or other devices that prohibit access to websites in the category that is denied by the network policy.

Acceptable Use Policies—Acceptable use policies should be annually reviewed by each user and signed to confirm that the users agree to the policies. These policies should include details regarding those activities that are permitted or not allowed. The point of the acceptable use policy is that the users have a clear understanding of what is expected regarding network activity and system use.

Standard Business Documents—Many standard documents are in use by companies. Some of these include service-level agreements (SLA). An SLA is a commitment to deliver a certain level of service.

For example, a service provider that offers wide area network services might guarantee a specific percentage of uptime as well as a committed throughput rate regarding the WAN circuits.

A memorandum of understanding (MOU) describes an agreement between two entities (two companies). It can be used instead of a formal contract when a handshake isn't enough.

Another form of an agreement between two parties could be a master service agreement (MSA). This is when both parties agree to terms that will govern future transactions and activities. When you have a master service agreement in place, details for future transactions and contracts do not need to be spelled out. Both parties can refer to the master service agreement.

When services are being performed, there is often a statement of work (SOW), which is a formal document that identifies the activities to be performed, the deliverables that are expected to be received, and the time frames.

Safety Practices

Care should be taken to ensure the safety of personnel, as well as the networks and the systems they support. This section summarizes the safety practices that should be considered.

Electrical Safety—Electricity is a common factor for the networks and systems, but it can also cause damage to those systems as well as employees and users when safety isn't practiced. Electrical systems should have proper grounding, and devices connecting into that electrical system should use the proper and approved cabling for the power. Planning should be done to allow for adequate power without overloading individual circuits or causing a potential hazardous situation.

ESD (Electrostatic Discharge)—ESD can damage electronic circuitry. Precautions to discharge any static buildup should be done before handling electronics. Wrist straps and other grounding mechanisms can help prevent buildup and harmful discharge.

Installation Safety—When network devices, equipment, or systems are being installed, safety is a high priority for the installer, for technicians who might use equipment later, and for the equipment itself. Care should be taken regarding lifting equipment, especially when working with heavy or awkward devices. Rack installation should be done in such a way that the racks will not tip over. The placement of network devices, cables, and systems should be done in such a way that they don't impose a hazard, including tripping issues. Proper training should be done to ensure safety when any of these tools are being used.

MSDS (Material Safety Data Sheet)—MSDS is a document that includes the information on how to safely work with a chemical product. For example, the MSDS for a pesticide has details regarding potential hazards of the pesticide and includes information above and beyond what was on the label of the pesticide itself. These are prepared by the supplier or manufacturer of the product that requires the MSDS.

Emergency Procedures—In the event of emergency, human life is the highest priority. Emergency procedures should be spelled out, periodically reviewed, and practiced. Some of the details might include an up-to-date building layout, fire escape plans, safety and emergency exits, emergency alert systems, and doors that either fail-open or fail-close in the event of a power failure. An exit door is an example of one that should fail-open, and a fire door, which is activated by a smoke detector, is an example of a door that should be designed to fail-close.

Fire Suppression—There are many types of fire suppression systems designed for different applications. In the data center it would not be wise to use water as a primary method for fire suppression because water would damage the equipment or possibly be ineffective in an electrical fire. Other options for fire suppression include chemicals that can extinguish the fire without the use of water. Fire suppression systems should be periodically inspected to verify that they are operational.

HVAC—Heating, ventilation, and air-conditioning (HVAC) systems involve airflow, which is consumed by humans. For that reason, care must be taken so that in the event of a fire or another contaminant to the air supply, the HVAC does not act as a catalyst in moving that contaminated air to multiple areas of the building. In addition, the servicing of an HVAC unit might involve chemicals, gas, and electricity. Proper safety practices should be followed with servicing any portion of the HVAC.

General Best Practices

This section discusses best practices regarding the installation and configuration of equipment in the appropriate locations, as well as change management.

Installation Best Practices—On each of the floors, a wiring closet, also referred to as an *intermediate distribution frame* (IDF), should be used to support a patch panel, cable trays, and access layer switches in that wiring closet. Near the data center at a central location in the building, a *main distribution frame* (MDF) can be used to manage the cables and connections between it and the intermediate description frame. Using cable trays and patch panels and proper labeling can assist in troubleshooting if problems arise with the physical cabling plant.

Proper power management should be observed. Having fault tolerance for power, which is referred to as *power redundancy*, should be implemented for critical systems. An uninterruptible power supply (UPS) helps protect against short-term power loss. A power converter might be needed to adapt the power to a system that uses a different level or category of power. Any circuits that are implemented as part of the power delivery should be protected against unauthorized access. When battery power, such as UPS, is used, a power inverter is being implemented that converts direct current to alternating current.

The placement of devices in the data center, in the wiring closet, and in the user areas should be done in such a way that system hazards can be avoided.

When network devices are powered on, they generate heat, including servers, workstations, routers, and switches. Proper airflow is critical to the cooling of most of these systems and should be planned appropriately. Regarding rack systems, a 19-inch-wide rack is a common format that supports most rack-mountable equipment, whether it's in the main distribution frame or in the intermediate distribution frame. There are many options regarding racks, including server rail racks, two-post racks, four-post racks, and freestanding racks. Care should be taken so that these racks are secured such that they will not tip over and will adequately support the gear that is placed inside them. Rack monitoring systems and rack security systems can also be used to secure the devices that are being kept in the racks.

Proper labeling is beneficial in troubleshooting and also helps in the implementation of network devices and cabling. You should consider using the following types of labeling:

- Port labeling
- System labeling
- Circuit labeling
- A common naming convention that can assist in identifying where devices are based on the names they have
- Patch panel labeling

Change Management—Change management is the process of identifying what needs to be done, obtaining authorization for the change, and documenting the change after it happens. Recommended details for a good change management system include the following:

- Documentation regarding the reason for change
- A change request form including the details regarding the configuration procedures
- A rollback process if the change is unsuccessful
- The potential impact
- How the users of the system will be notified regarding the change that's happening

One of the benefits of having a very well-defined rollback process is that if a change is made—for example, a new application is installed—but then there's a problem, the rollback can then be easily implemented.

One of the key factors in any upgrade or change is to test it in a lab environment before putting it into the production network.

Part of change control also involves an approval process by management.

Some organizations have a specified maintenance window, which is a time once a week or twice a month when the network is expected to be down (usually during off-peak hours) during which maintenance can be performed. Communication and documentation regarding changes, which includes notification of changes to those systems and users that are impacted, should be part of a formal change control process. Included in the documentation for change control should be any related network configurations, including backups, additions to the network, and physical location changes such as a switch or router or server being moved to a different rack or location.

Ports and Protocols

Applications often have well-known ports that networked devices, including servers, might have open as listening ports when those associated services are running. This section includes details regarding many well-known ports and the protocols that use them. Table 22-4 shows protocols and ports that you should memorize.

TCP—TCP is a connection-oriented Layer 4 protocol in the TCP/IP protocol suite. It supports connection-oriented sessions. This is accomplished by using synchronization and acknowledgments as part of the communications to verify whether the data has been received. If the data did not make it to the destination, TCP can compensate by resending it.

UDP—UDP is a connectionless protocol at Layer 4 in the TCP/IP protocol suite. It has less overhead than TCP because it does not use synchronization requests or acknowledgments to confirm that data was received correctly.

Table 22-4 *Protocols with Well-Known Ports*

Protocol	Description	TCP Port	UDP Port
HTTP	Hypertext Transfer Protocol: Retrieves content from a web server	80	
HTTPS	Hypertext Transfer Protocol Secure: Used to securely retrieve content from a web server	443	
NetBIOS	Network Basic Input/Output System: Provides network communication services for LANs that use NetBIOS	139	137 138
POP3	Post Office Protocol Version 3: Retrieves e-mail from an e-mail server	110	
IMAP	Internet Message Access Protocol: Retrieves e-mail from an e-mail server	143	
SMTP	Simple Mail Transfer Protocol: Used for sending e-mail	25	

Protocol	Description	TCP Port	UDP Port
SIP	Session Initiation Protocol: Used to create and end sessions for one or more media connections, including voice over IP calls	5060 5061	5060 5061
MGCP	Media Gateway Control Protocol: Used as a call control and communication protocol for voice over IP networks	2427 2727	2427 2727
RTP	Real-time Transport Protocol: Used for delivering media-based data over networks, such as voice over IP	5004 5005	5004 5005
H.323	A signaling protocol used to provide multimedia communications over a network	1720	
FTP	File Transfer Protocol: Transfers files with a remote host (typically requires authentication of user credentials)	20, 21	
SNMP	Simple Network Management Protocol: Used to monitor and manage network devices		161
SSH	Secure Shell: Securely connect to a remote host (typically via a terminal emulator)	22	
Telnet	Used to connect to a remote host (typically via a terminal emulator)	23	
DNS	Domain Name System: Resolves domain names to corresponding IP addresses	53	53
DHCP	Dynamic Host Configuration Protocol: Dynamically assigns IP address information (for example, IP address, subnet mask, DNS server's IP address, and default gateway's IP address) to a network device		67 68
TFTP	Trivial File Transfer Protocol: Transfers files with a remote host (does not require authentication of user credentials)		69
SMB	Server Message Block: Used to share files, printers, and other network resources	445	
RDP	Remote Desktop Protocol: A Microsoft protocol that enables a user to view and control the desktop of a remote computer	3389	

To receive your 10% off
Exam Voucher, register
your product at:

www.pearsonitcertification.com/register

and follow the instructions.